The Employment Law Checklist

Seventh Edition

by

Erich Suter
BA, MIOSH, FIPD
of the Middle Temple, Barrister

Principal, Industrial Relations Workshop

Institute of Personnel and Development

First published 1981 as *Legislation for Personnel Managers:
A checklist* by the Institute of Personnel Management

Reprinted 1982; revised 2nd edition 1982; revised 3rd edition
1985; revised 4th edition 1990; revised 5th edition 1992; revised
6th edition 1997; revised 7th edition 2000.

© Institute of Personnel and Development as successors in
business to the Institute of Personnel Management 1981, 1982,
1985, 1990, 1992, 1997, 2000.

All rights reserved. No part of this publication may be
reproduced, stored in an information storage and retrieval
system, or transmitted in any form or by any means, electronic,
mechanical, photocopying, recording or otherwise, without
written permission of the Institute of Personnel and
Development, IPD House, Camp Road, Wimbledon, London,
SW19 4UX.

Phototypeset by Fakenham Photosetting Ltd, Fakenham,
Norfolk.
Printed in Great Britain by
The Short Run Press, Exeter

British Library Cataloguing in Publication Data
A catalogue record for this book is available from the British
Library

ISBN 0–85292–849–1

Throughout this book the pronoun 'he' should be taken to
include 'she' where appropriate.

The views expressed in this book are the author's own and may not
necessarily reflect those of the IPD.

INSTITUTE OF PERSONNEL
AND DEVELOPMENT

IPD House, Camp Road, London SW19 4UX
Tel: 020-8971 9000   Fax: 020-8263 3333
Registered office as above. Registered Charity No. 1038333
A company limited by guarantee. Registered in England No. 2931892

The Employment Law Checklist

Erich Suter

LIVERPOOL JMU LIBRARY

3 1111 00922 0979

Erich Suter, BA, MISOSH, FIPD, barrister of the Middle Temple, is the senior employment lawyer at the Industrial Relations Workshop and was for many years the IPD's Employment Law Adviser.

LIVERPOOL JOHN MOORES UNIVERSITY
Aldham Robarts L.R.C.
TEL. 051 231 3701/3634

The Institute of Personnel and Development is the leading publisher
of books and reports for personnel and training professionals,
students, and all those concerned with the effective management
and development of people at work. For details of all our titles,
please contact the Publishing Department:

tel. 020-8263 3387

fax 020-8263 3850

e-mail publish@ipd.co.uk

The catalogue of all IPD titles can be viewed on the IPD website:

http://www.ipd.co.uk/publications

Contents

Introduction

This edition of *The Employment Law Checklist* revises and updates previous editions, the last of which was published in 1997. On this occasion there have been significant changes in the law, something to be expected with the advent of a new government. There has also been a further shift towards making law by statutory regulations rather than by statutes; both directly – as in the case of the Working Time Regulations and indirectly – as in the case of the Employment Relations Act 1999, which was passed as a bare shell, left to be legislated by way of Regulations (most of which have yet to be made). Not surprisingly this is reflected by a shift in the balance of the new material in this edition. For the first time, of the 30 major pieces of new legislation covered only 15 are statutes and the other 15 are statutory instruments (and this does not take into account minor sets of Regulations and Orders which are dealt with, in the body of the text, only under the relevant legislation which they amend or bring into force). It should be borne in mind that this book is, and is intended to be, no more than a 'thumbnail' guide to employment legislation. Much of the statutory material covering employment matters, eg health and safety at work, is contained in statutory instruments and other delegated legislation, supported by codes of practice. Even with the continuing increase in coverage of statutory instruments in this edition, much of the material that is dealt with in Regulations is of more restricted application or is relevant to only a small part of industry and has therefore not been included. Apart from delegated legislation, a considerable part of the law surrounding employment has not been codified into Acts of Parliament and many fundamental parts of the law (eg contract, negligence, etc.) remain the province of the common law (or 'judge-made law'). For the above reasons, readers should rely on this guide merely as a starting point to ensure that they are aware of the more basic requirements of the law relating to employment and to update their knowledge of those requirements. Those with specific legal problems are recommended to take professional legal advice.*

The 'new format' for the checklist (first adopted for the 4th edition in 1990) has been maintained with a slight modification and the layout is as follows:

1. Chronological list of legislation – lists in date order all the legislation detailed in Part 2.

2. Alphabetical list of legislation – gives brief outline of the contents, scope and effect of each Act.

3. The index – designed to help readers follow particular topics through the various bits of legislation relating to them.

The recommended reading list has been taken out for two reasons. First the early

---

* The author's consultancy, Industrial Relations Workshop, can be contacted for professional advice and assistance with employment tribunal cases, appeals to EAT, drawing up contracts of employment and handbooks etc. on 020-8979 1020 (e-mail http://www.enquiries@*i-r-w*.com).

retirement of Marilyn Arnott, IPD Librarian, who prepared the bibliography for the previous editions, but also the fact that in many of the subject areas there have been recent innovations, which mean that there will be a rush of new books to the market early in 2000 to deal with these items. At the time of writing these books are not yet available.

As always, the IPD library will be keeping up to date with new publications and the library staff will be pleased to help members with any queries.

Acknowledgements

The extracts from the IPM Digest/PM Plus are reproduced by kind permission of the Institute of Personnel and Development.

Dedication

This book is dedicated to the memory of Deirdre Gill, who was IPM Assistant Director, Information and Advisory Services, a friend and mentor.

Part 1
Chronological List of Legislation

1814	Apprentices Act
1831 to 1940	Truck Acts (repealed)
1870	Apportionment Act
1913	Trade Union Act (repealed/consolidated)
1919	Sex Disqualification (Removal) Act
1920	Employment of Women, Young Persons and Children Act
1933 to 1969	Children and Young Persons Acts
1936	Public Health Act
1938	Young Persons (Employment) Act (repealed)
	Disabled Persons (Employment) Acts 1944 and 1958 (employment provisions repealed)
1944 and 1973	Education Acts (largely repealed)
1950 to 1965	Shop Acts
1960	Payment of Wages Act (repealed)
1961	Factories Act
1963	Offices, Shops and Railway Premises Act
1964	Industrial Training Act
	Trade Union (Amalgamations) Act (repealed/consolidated)
	Young Persons (Employment Act) (repealed)
1969	Employers' Liability (Defective Equipment) Act
	Employers' Liability (Compulsory Insurance) Act
	Family Law Reform Act
1970	Equal Pay Act
1971	Attachment of Earnings Act
	Banking and Financial Dealings Act
	Fire Precautions Act
	Immigration Act
1972	Children Act
	Employment Medical Advisory Services Act
	European Communities Act – Treaty of Rome
1973	Education (Work Experience) Act (repealed)
	Employment Agencies Act
	Employment of Children Act (overtaken by Education Act 1996)
	Employment and Training Act
1974	Health and Safety at Work etc. Act
	Rehabilitation of Offenders Act
	Trade Union and Labour Relations Act (repealed/consolidated)
1975	Employment Protection Act (repealed/consolidated)
	Industry Act
	Sex Discrimination Act
	Social Security Act (repealed/consolidated)

	Social Security Pensions Act
1976	Race Relations Act
	Trade Union and Labour Relations (Amendment) Act (repealed/consolidated)
1977	Job Release Act
	Patents Act
	Unfair Contract Terms Act
	Safety Representatives and Safety Committees Regulations 1977 (SI 1977 No. 500)
1978	Employment Protection (Consolidation) Act (repealed/ consolidated)
	Employment (Continental Shelf) Act
	Employment Subsidies Act
1979	Wages Council Act (repealed)
1980	Employment Act (repealed/consolidated)
	Social Security (No. 2) Act (repealed/consolidated)
	Industry Act
	Reserve Forces Act
1981	Industry Act
	Employment and Training Act
	Transfer of Undertakings (Protection of Employment) Regulations
1982	Industrial Training Act
	Agricultural Training Board Act
	Employment Act (repealed/consolidated)
	Oil and Gas (Enterprise) Act
	Social Security and Housing Benefits Act (largely repealed/ consolidated)
	Social Security (Medical Evidence, Claims and Payments) Amendment Regulations
1983	Equal Pay (Amendment) Regulations
1984	Data Protection Act (repealed)
	Health and Social Security Act (largely repealed/consolidated)
	Trade Union Act (repealed/consolidated)
1985	Companies Act
	Insolvency Act
	Reserve Forces (Safeguard of Employment) Act
	Social Security Act (largely repealed/consolidated)
1986	Insolvency Act
	Sex Discrimination Act
	Social Security Act (repealed/consolidated)
	Wages Act (repealed/consolidated)
1987	Fire Safety and Safety of Places of Sport Act
1988	Access to Medical Reports Act

Industrial Tribunals Extension of Jurisdiction (England and Wales) Order 1994 (SI 1994/1623)/(Scotland – SI 1994/1624) (renamed as Employment Tribunals Extension of Jurisdiction (England and Wales) Order 1994)

Race Relations (Remedies) Act

Social Security (Incapacity for Work) Act

Statutory Sick Pay Act

Sunday Trading Act (repealed/consolidated)

1995   Collective Redundancies and Transfer of Undertakings (Protection of Employment) (Amendment) Regulations SI 1995/2587

Disability Discrimination Act

Job Seekers Act

Pensions Act

1996   Asylum and Immigration Act

Armed Forces Act 1996

Education Act 1996

Employment Rights Act

Employment Tribunals Act

Employment Tribunals Rules of Procedure (Amendment) Rules 1996

Finance Act 1996

Industrial Tribunals Rules of Procedure (Amendment) Rules 1996 (SI 1996 No. 1757) (renamed as Employment Tribunals Rules of Procedure (Amendment) Rules 1996)

Industrial Tribunals Act (renamed as Employment Tribunals Act)

Reserve Forces Act

Health and Safety (Consultation with Employees) Regulations 1996 (SI 1996 No. 1513)

1997   Education Act 1997

Finance Act 1997

Fire Precautions (Workplace) Regulations 1997

The Health and Safety (Young Persons) Regulations 1997 (SI 1997 No. 135)

Police Act

Police (Health and Safety) Act 1997

Protection from Harassment Act 1997

1998   Children (Protection at Work) Regulations 1998 (SI 1998 No. 276)

Data Protection Act 1998

Deregulation (Deduction from Pay of Union Subscriptions) Order 1998 (SI 1998 No. 1529)

Disability Discrimination (Exemption for Small Employers) Order 1998 (SI 1998 No. 2618)

Employment Rights (Dispute Resolution) Act 1998

Human Rights Act 1998

The Lifting Operation and Lifting Equipment Regulations 1998 (SI 1998 No. 2307)

Provision of Work Equipment Regulations 1998 (SI 1998 No. 2306)

Public Interest Disclosure Act 1998

Social Security (Welfare to Work) Regulations 1998 (SI 1998 No. 2231)

Teaching and Higher Education Act 1998

The Working Time Regulations 1998 (SI 1998 No. 1833)

1999   Collective Redundancies and Transfer of Undertakings (Protection of Employment) (Amendment Regulations) 1999 (SI 1999 No. 1925)

Control of Substances Hazardous to Health Regulations 1999 (S1 1999 No. 437)

Disability Rights Commission Act 1999

Employment Relations Act 1999

National Minimum Wage Act 1998 and National Minimum Wage Regulations 1999 (SI 1999 No. 584)

Redundancy Payments (Continuity of Employment in Local Government etc.) (Modification) Order 1999

Sex Discrimination (Gender Reassignment) Regulations 1999

Unfair Dismissal and Statement of Reasons for Dismissal (Variation of Qualifying Period) Order 1999 (SI 1999 No. 1436)

List of abbreviations

EPCA	Employment Protection (Consolidation) Act 1992
ERA	Employment Rights Act 1996
HASWA	Health and Safety at Work etc. Act 1974
TULRA	Trade Union and Labour Relations (Consolidation) Act 1992
TURERA	Trade Union Reform and Employment Rights Act 1993

Part 2
Alphabetical List of Legislation

1 Access to Health Records Act 1990 (largely repealed and with its effects subsumed by the Data Protection Act 1998)

This Act came into force on 1 November 1991. It has been more or less repealed for employment purposes by the Data Protection Act 1998. At the time of writing, however, the Secretary of State's powers to make Regulations under the Data Protection Act 1998 have not been exercised so it is difficult to know what restrictions are likely to be put in place to prevent individuals from finding out information about their health which might harm them.

It is also notable that the definition of 'Care' in the 1990 Act, which includes any examination of a patient without requiring that that examination be for purposes of medical treatment, which is the more restrictive definition of 'care' in the Access to Medical Reports Act 1988 (see 2.1 below), is not repealed. There is no definition of 'care' under the Data Protection Act 1998.

2 Access to Medical Reports Act 1988

Amended by the Data Protection Act 1998.

This Act came into force on 1 January 1989. It relates to medical reports obtained for the purposes of employment (or of insurance).

2.1 Definitions

The Act defines a medical report as a report
- relating to the physical or mental health of the individual; which
- is prepared by a medical practitioner who is or who has been responsible for the clinical care of the individual; and care is defined by the Act as including examination, investigation or diagnosis *for the purposes of* or in connection with *any form of medical treatment.*

Where a one-off medical report is sought from a specialist or from a company doctor who has not been involved in the clinical care of the employee the Act will not apply.

2.2 Notification to employee

Section 3 of the Act provides that no employer/prospective employer may ask a medical practitioner for a medical report, covered by the Act, in respect of an employee unless the individual is notified that the employer proposes to make the application and the individual has notified the employer that he consents to the application being made.

The notification given by an employer must inform the employee of the various rights provided for by the Act, ie:

(a) *The employee's right to withhold his consent to the making of such an application*

The employee can withhold his consent to any application being made by an employer for such a medical report.

(b) *The employee's right to be given access to the medical practitioner's report before it is supplied to the employer*

If the employee consents to the report being made and asks that he be given access to it, under this provision, then the medical practitioner must be informed by the employer of the employee's wish to have access to the report before it is given to the employer.

Under the terms of the Act, however, it appears to be for the employee to make his own arrangements with the medical practitioner to obtain access to the report.

Whether or not the employee asks for and obtains inspection of the report is significant, since a number of the rights in relation to the report depend upon his having had access to the report.

If the employee asks for access to the report then the medical practitioner may not pass on the report to the employer unless the employee has either been given access to it (and certain other requirements have been met – see below) or 21 days have passed and he has not made arrangements to obtain access to the report.

(c) *The employee's right to notify the medical practitioner directly that he wishes to have access to the report*

If the individual employee consents to the report being applied for, but does not say that he wants to have access to it before it is passed to his employer, he is allowed to ask the medical practitioner directly to give him access to the report. In such cases, again, the medical practitioner may not pass on the report to the employer unless the employee has either been given access to it (and certain other requirements have been met – see below) or 21 days have passed and the employee has not made arrangements to obtain access to the report.

(d) *The employee's right to be given access by a medical practitioner to any medical reports relating to him and supplied by the medical practitioner, for employment purposes, within the previous six months*

If the employee has consented to any report being applied for, he may ask the medical practitioner to give him access to any such report that he has supplied in the previous six months. (This applies only to reports made after the Act came into force on 1 January 1989.)

(e) *The employee's right to refuse his consent to the report being given to his employer*

If the employee has had access to the report then the report can be passed on to his employer only if he consents to this being done.

Once the employee has consented to the report being sought then the individual generally only has further rights under the Act if he has had access to the report. There are two exceptions to this limitation:

- the employee retains the right to access a report made within the previous six months; or

- where the report is one to which he has not been allowed access, despite asking for it, because the medical practitioner has refused access on specified grounds (see below). If the whole of the report is covered by these grounds, so that the employee is not entitled to access to any of it, the report may still be passed on to his employer only with his express consent.

(f) *The employee's right to request the medical practitioner, in writing, before giving his consent to the report being supplied, to amend any part of the report that the individual considers to be misleading or incorrect*

The employee may ask the medical practitioner to amend any part/s of a report to which he has had access that he considers to be incorrect or misleading. The medical practitioner may amend the report to the extent that he is prepared so to do. If he is not prepared to amend it, or if he is not prepared to amend it as extensively as the individual might wish, then the individual may ask that a statement of his views be attached to the report. Any such request must also be made in writing.

2.3　Grounds on which a medical practitioner may refuse an individual access to a medical report

A medical practitioner may refuse an individual access to all or parts of a medical report where he considers that disclosure of the report, or of those parts:

- would be likely to 'cause serious harm to the physical or mental health of the individual or others'; or
- would indicate the intentions of the medical practitioner in relation to that individual; or
- would be likely to reveal information about another person without that person's consent; or
- would be likely to reveal the identity of another person (ie a non-health professional) who has given information to the practitioner about the individual – again, unless that person consents to the disclosure.

In any such case the medical practitioner must inform the individual that he considers that the above criteria apply either to all or to parts of the report. In such cases the individual is entitled to have access only to any parts of the report that are not covered by the above prohibitions on disclosure. If the whole of the report is covered by these prohibitions, then the employee is not entitled to access to any of it. However, any such report may be passed on to his employer, assuming that the employee originally asked for access to it, only with the employee's express consent.

2.4　Enforcement of the Act

Enforcement of the Act is through the county court (sheriff's court in Scotland). The Act simply provides that if it appears to the court that any person has failed or is likely to fail to comply with any part of the Act then the court may order that they do comply. Any failure to comply with such an order would, of course, amount to contempt of court.

3 Agricultural Training Board Act 1982

Amended by Employment Act 1989.

Repeals most of the Training Act 1964 as it applied to the Agricultural Training Board and part of Employment and Training Act 1973.

Consolidates the law relating to the Agricultural Training Board.

4 Apportionment Act 1870

The effect of ss 2 and 5 is that 'salaries ... shall be considered as accruing from day to day, and shall be apportioned in respect of time accordingly'. It is undecided whether or not 'wages' accrue on a daily basis.

5 Apprentices Act 1814

The effect of this Act is that a contract of apprenticeship must be written. If it is not, it will take effect as a contract of employment.

NB A contract of apprenticeship is defined as being a contract of employment for employment protection purposes (see s 230 Employment Rights Act 1996).

5A Armed Forces Act 1996

Amends Equal Pay Act 1970, Rehabilitation of Offenders Act 1974, Sex Discrimination Act 1975 and Race Discrimination Act 1976.

Makes various provisions extending the protection of the equal pay and the sex and race discrimination legislation to complaints arising from service in the armed forces; subject to a requirement that the complaint must be taken up using internal machinery before a complaint is made to an employment tribunal. The provisions of the Rehabilitation of Offenders Act 1974 are also extended to encompass certain sentences imposed by Courts Martial.

6 Attachment of Earnings Act 1971

Empowers a court to order that a judgment debt be paid directly by the employer, from the employee's earnings, to the court.

7 Asylum and Immigration Act 1996

Amends the Immigration Act 1971.

For employment purposes, the most important effect of this Act is that it makes it an offence for an employer to employ someone who is not entitled to be in and to work in the UK.

7.1 The offence

(a) An employer commits an offence if:
- (i)   he employs a person of 16 or over (the 'employee')
- (ii) the employee is subject to immigration control; and
    - the employee does not have current valid leave to be in the UK; or
    - the employee's leave is subject to a condition which stops him from

taking up that employment. (NB: The reference to 'that employment' is important since an employee who has a work permit, for example, will be entitled to work in the employment to which the permit relates, but not in any other job.)

(b) In certain cases, even where the employee, prima facie, is not entitled to be in, or to work in, the UK an employer may nonetheless employ him. The three situations in which this is permissible were introduced by the Immigration (Restrictions on Employment) Order 1996 (SI 1996 No. 3225)

    (i) where an employee, having made a claim for asylum which is still under consideration, has been given written permission to work by the Home Office

    (ii) where the employee has an appeal pending under Part II of the Immigration Act 1971 – provided that before the appeal was made the employee was entitled to work in the UK

    (iii) if the employee is entitled to work under the Immigration Rules.

7.2 The defence

An employer will have a defence to a potential prosecution for employing someone who is not entitled to be or to work in the UK if before that person's employment began:

(a) the employer was shown a document that appeared to relate to the employee in question (ie it appeared to be both a genuine document and to relate to the employee)

(b) the document was of a description specified by the Secretary of State as being appropriate for these purposes (see 7.3 below)

(c) the employer either kept the document itself or a copy of it. (A copy can be either a paper copy or a copy kept on a WORM CD, ie a Write Once Read Many times CD. This means that the CD can be written on only once so that a true, unalterable copy is kept); and

(d) the employer did not know that employing the employee would be unlawful under these provisions.

7.3 Acceptable documents

The Home Office has issued a guide to employers dealing with the requirements under these provisions. A full list of the types of document that are acceptable for purposes of the defence in 7.2 above is contained in the guide which has been sent to all employers. The main documents are as follows:

(a) Usually employers will be provided by new employees with a 'documented National Insurance number' (an official document on which the person's National Insurance number is stated). This could be:

    • a document issued by a previous employer, such as a P45, a pay slip or a P60

    • a document issued by the Inland Revenue, the Benefits Agency, the Contributions Agency or the Employment Service (or their Northern Ireland equivalents) such as a NINO card (the newer plastic cards or the older-style cards) or a letter issued by one of the government bodies mentioned above. It should be noted that a document showing a National Insurance number with a 'TN' prefix is a temporary National Insurance number and is not acceptable.

(b) a passport showing that the person is a British or EU citizen or which has a stamp on it showing that the person has a right to be or to remain in the UK

(c) naturalisation papers

(d) a work permit or a letter from the immigration authorities saying that the person has a right to work in the UK.

7.4　Race discrimination

It is obviously important that all job applicants are treated the same so that there are no accusations or feelings that people are being discriminated against on grounds of their race. One way of dealing with this is to ask for the same documents from all those who are going to be offered a job. Employers may have their own list of documents which all employees are required to produce. These might include, for example, a P45, P60, other documented NI number, passport, etc.

7.5　Further information

(a) There is a helpline which is available to anyone with a query on these requirements – 020-8649 7878. The Employer's Guide is also available on the Internet at http://www.open.gov.uk/home_off/ind.htm

(b) The CRE has issued provisional guidance on good practice for employers in dealing with these requirements.

8　Banking and Financial Dealings Act 1971

Amended by Employment Act 1989.

Repeals previous legislation relating to bank holidays and substitutes a schedule of bank holidays.

9　Children and Young Persons Acts 1933–1969, Children Act 1972, Employment of Women, Young Persons and Children Act 1920

Amended by Employment Act 1989. The 1933 Act is amended by Manual Handling Operations Regulations 1992 SI 1992/2793 and by the Children (Protection at Work) Regulations 1998 (SI 1998 No. 276).

These Acts restrict the employment of children. They are repealed by the Employment Act 1989 insofar as they restricted the employment of women and young persons and modified by the Children (Protection at Work) Regulations 1998 (SI 1998 No. 276) as far as the employment of children is concerned.

9A　Children (Protection at Work) Regulations 1998 (SI 1998 No. 276)

Amend Children and Young Persons Act 1933 and 1963. These Regulations were brought in to give effect to the 1994 EC Directive on the Protection of Young People at Work (94/33/EC).

The lowest age at which a child can be employed is raised from 13 to 14.

The prohibition against employing children on work that might harm them is replaced with a prohibition against them undertaking anything other than 'light work'. Light work is work that does not jeopardise a child's safety, health, development, attendance at school or participation in work experience.

Hours of work and required rest breaks for children at work are also brought into line with those required by the Directive, and a requirement is introduced that a child must have at least one two-week period in his school holidays when he does no work.

The requirement to obtain a local authority licence before children can take part in public performances for profit or go abroad to perform for profit is extended to children taking part in sports or modelling for money whether in this country or abroad.

10   Collective Redundancies and Transfer of Undertakings (Protection of Employment) (Amendment) Regulations SI 1995/2587

Amend the Employment Protection (Consolidation) Act 1978 (now consolidated into ERA), TULRA and Transfer of Undertakings (Protection of Employment) Regulations 1981.

These regulations provide for representation by employee representatives as an alternative to trade union representation in relation to:

(a) consultation about proposed redundancies (see also 102.10); and

(b) consultation about transfers of undertakings (see also 105.1).

10A   Collective Redundancies and Transfer of Undertakings (Protection of Employment) (Amendment Regulations) 1999 (SI 1999 No. 1925) and Transfer of Undertakings (Protection of Employment) (Amendment) Regulations 1999 (SI 1999 No. 2402)

The Collective Redundancies and Transfer of Undertakings (Protection of Employment) (Amendment Regulations) 1999 amend Transfer of Undertakings (Protection of Employment) Regulations 1981 and Trade Union, Labour Relations (Consolidation) Act 1992 and Employment Rights Act 1996. The Regulations came into effect on 28 July 1999. They were almost immediately amended by the Transfer of Undertakings (Protection of Employment) (Amendment) Regulations 1999 (SI 1999 No. 2402) to correct a minor drafting fault in the first Regulations.

(a) *Collective redundancies*

    i)   **Extending consultation requirements to those who are not going to be dismissed**

        Where an employer is proposing to dismiss 20 or more employees at the same establishment within a period of 90 days, the requirement for consultation is extended so that the employer must now consult with the appropriate representatives not merely of those whom it is proposed to dismiss, as was previously the case, but also with representatives of all those who may be affected

- by the proposed dismissals; or
- by measures taken in connection with those dismissals.

ii) **A requirement to consult with recognised trade unions if there are any**
The ability of the employer to chose whether to consult with a recognised trade union or employee representatives is removed. The employee must consult with any trade union that is recognised. If there is no recognised trade union the employer must consult with employee representatives.

iii) **Employee representatives**
Employee representatives for these purposes may be:

- representatives who were appointed or elected by the affected employees for a reason other than redundancy consultation. This can happen only if, having regard to the purposes for which they were elected and to the way in which they were elected or appointed, they can be considered to have the authority of the employees in question to receive information and to be consulted about the redundancy on their behalf
- representatives appointed or elected by the affected employees specifically for the redundancy consultation. Any such election must satisfy the following specific requirements:
  - *the employer must ensure that the election is fair;
  - the employer must decide on the number of representatives to be elected so that there are enough representatives to represent the interests of all the affected employees. In deciding on the number of representatives the employer must take into account
    - the number; and
    - types of employees affected;
  - the employer must decide whether the employee representatives should represent just one class of employees or all the employees;
  - before the election the employer must decide for how long the representatives are to hold office (it must be long enough for them to be given the information required by statute and to complete the statutory consultation);
  - *the candidates for election must themselves be affected by the redundancy at the date of election;
  - *no affected employee may be unreasonably excluded from standing for election;
  - all employees who are affected at the date of election must be entitled to vote;

- all affected employees must be allowed to vote for as many candidates as represent them or the particular class of employee that they fall into;
- *the election must be by secret ballot;
- *the votes must be counted accurately.
- If an employee representative, elected under the above criteria, ceases to act as such then there must be an election to replace him which meets the requirements that are asterisked in the above list

iv) **If the employees fail to elect representatives**
- if the affected employees fail to elect representatives within a reasonable time then the information required to be given to representatives to start consultation under s 188(4) TULR(C)A is to be given individually to each of the affected employees.

v) Those who can claim a protective award (ie: an award to compensate each employee for a number of days to reflect the lack of consultation) are amended in line with the additional duties that have been imposed on the employer under these Regulations. Who can bring a complaint still depends on the nature of the employer's particular failure in relation to the appointment of employee representatives or consultation requirements.
- In the case of any failure relating to election of an employee representative, any of the employees who are affected by the redundancy or dismissed as redundant can present a complaint
- In the case of any other failure relating to employee representatives, the employee representative to whom the failure relates can present a complaint
- in the case of any failure to fulfil any requirement relating to a trade union representative, the trade union is the appropriate complainant
- in any other case an affected employee or one who has been or may be dismissed as redundant can complain.

vi) **The Regulations change the burden of proof in relation to two situations.** In both burden is put on to the employer:
- In relation to the question of whether or not the employee representative was 'appropriate' the employer must prove that the employee representative had authority to represent the affected employees; and
- It is for the employer to prove that the requirements concerning the election of employee representatives have been complied with

vii) **The lower maximum level of protective award is revoked.**
- If the tribunal finds a complaint well founded it can make a protective award. This is payable to each of the employees in respect of whom there has been a failure in relation to employee representatives or consultation. The protected period still continues for such time as the tribunal considers just and equitable having regard to the seriousness of the employer's default, subject to a maximum of 90 days regardless of the number of employees made redundant. The erstwhile lower limit

of 30 days for cases where between 30 and 100 employees were made
redundant has been removed by the Regulations.

(b) *Transfers of undertakings*

   i)   The requirements concerning:
- the need to consult a recognised trade union, rather than employee representatives;
- employee representatives and their elections;
- the need to consult employees directly in the absence of any employee representatives;
- who may present a claim in respect of any failure by the employer; and
- the reversal of the burden of proof;

      are all the same as in relation to Collective redundancies (above).

   ii) The maximum award that a tribunal can make if the employer has failed to meet any of the election or consultation requirements in relation to the transfer of an undertaking is increased from four weeks' to 13 weeks' pay.

11   Companies Acts 1985 and 1989

11A   Companies Act 1985

The Companies Act 1985 is a consolidation of the previous Companies Acts. The Companies Act 1985 is of great importance to the employment, duties and liabilities of company directors.

Matters of particular concern in the personnel field:

11A.1 The Act obliges companies to keep a copy or memorandum of their directors' contracts of employment for inspection by members of the company (ie shareholders).

11A.2 A contract of employment with a director that is to be for more than five years and which includes any restriction on the company's ability to terminate the contract by notice, may be made only if approved by a general meeting of the company following due notification of the terms of the agreement.

11A.3 The Act puts directors under a duty to perform their functions so as to promote the interests of the company's employees as well as its shareholders. It also includes within the powers of a company, where this is not specified, a power for the company to make adequate provision for its employees (or those of a subsidiary company) where the company is winding up or being transferred.

11A.4 The Act requires certain matters to be disclosed in directors' reports where the average number of employees in a company in each week of the relevant financial year is more than 250. These are:

  (a) the policy that has been applied in relation to disabled employees during that year:
- for giving full and fair consideration to applications for employment from disabled people

- for continuing the employment of and retraining of those who become disabled while in the company's employment
- for training, career development and promotion of disabled employees generally within the company.

(b) the action taken during that year to introduce, maintain or develop arrangements aimed at:
  - systematically providing employees with information on matters of concern to them as employees
  - consulting employees/their representatives on a regular basis so that employees' views can be taken into account in making decisions that are likely to affect employees' interests
  - encouraging employee involvement in the company's performance through employee share schemes or by other means
  - achieving a common awareness on the part of all employees of the financial and economic factors affecting the performance of the company

11B   Companies Act 1989

Amends the Companies Act 1985 to require that all elements of remuneration paid to directors and any payments for loss of office be disclosed. This applies whether the payments are made by the company itself or by a holding or subsidiary company.

12   Company Securities (Insider Dealing) Act 1985

Repealed and replaced by Part V Criminal Justice Act 1993 (see below, Section 15).

13   Computer Misuse Act 1990

Makes it a criminal offence for a person knowingly to try to gain unauthorised access to a computer program or to any data held on a computer. The Act also makes it an offence to try to modify any of the contents of a computer without authority.

13A   Control of Substances Hazardous to Health Regulations 1999 (S1 1999 No. 437)

These Regulations revoke and re-enact, with minor modifications, the Control of Substances Hazardous to Health Regulations 1994 (SI 1994/3246) as amended over the years. The Regulations amend the Health and Safety at Work etc. Act 1974.

(a) *Protection against substances hazardous to health*
  - Duties are imposed on employers to protect employees and others who may be exposed to substances hazardous to health.
  - Personal protective equipment must provided by an employer to comply with the Personal Protective Equipment (EC Directive) Regulations; and
  - A duty is placed on employees to use any protective equipment provided and any controls put in place by the employer to protect them from such exposure.

- Maximum exposure levels to substances may be set as approved by the Health and Safety Commission

(b) *Import of substances hazardous to health*

The Regulations prohibit the import into the United Kingdom of certain substances and articles from outside the European Economic Area.

14   Copyright, Designs and Patents Act 1988

Repeals the Copyright Act 1956 and consolidates the law of copyright.

14.1 Determines the ownership of the copyright of literary, dramatic or other artistic works and provides that the copyright in such a work created by an employee in the course of his employment belongs to the employer, subject to any agreement to the contrary.

14.2 The copyright in anything done outside the course of the employee's duties belongs to the employee.

14.3 The ownership of a copyright may be determined by contract.

14.4 Computer software is subject to copyright.

15   Criminal Justice Act 1993

Part V repeals and replaces the Company Securities (Insider Dealing) Act 1985.

15.1 Prohibits any individual from knowingly dealing in securities of any company when he has information 'as an insider'. It also prohibits him from encouraging anyone else to deal in such securities or disclosing the information which he has 'as an insider' to anyone else, other than in the proper performance of his employment or profession.

15.2 'Inside information' is information which:
- relates to particular securities
- is specific
- is unpublished
- would be likely, if published, to have a significant effect on the price of any securities.

15.3 A person has information 'as an insider', *inter alia*, if
- it is inside information; and
- he has obtained it through his employment; or
- he has obtained it from someone who obtained it through his (the other person's) employment.

16   Data Protection Act 1984 (repealed)
16A   Data Protection Act 1998

Repeals the Data Protection Act 1984, Access to Personal Files Act 1987. Amends Access to Medical Reports Act 1988 and Access to Health Records Act 1990.

The Act comes into force on 1 March 2000

Provides for the compulsory registration of users of personal data and for individual access to personal data concerning the individual. It extends the protection offered by the 1984 Act, which was concerned only with computerised information to paper information as well as extending the level of protection of personal data. The Act also provides for compensation for misuse of personal data and for compensation to data subjects for inaccuracies. The main framework of the Act is as follows:

16A.1 Definitions

Data is information that is:

(a) recorded in a form in which it is or is intended to be processed automatically;
(b) held in a filing system which is structured in a way that information concerning individuals is readily accessible (this will encompass paper personnel systems) – although paper filing systems are subject to transitional relief until 2001 or 2007 (see Section 16 A.3); or
(c) part of an 'accessible record', most important of which are health records. A health record is one that has been made by a health professional in connection with the care of an individual and which concerns that individual's physical or mental state. Although 'health professional' is defined by the Act, 'care' is not. This is likely to lead to some difficulties since 'care' has been given different meanings in the Access to Health Records Act 1990 (see 1.1 above) and the Access to Medical Reports Act 1988 (see 2.1 above).

Processing is more widely defined under these provisions than it was under the 1984 Act. Processing now means obtaining, recording or holding information or carrying out any operations on the information or data, including by organising, adapting, or altering the data; retrieving or consulting it or disclosing or making it available.

Personal data is data that relates to a living individual who is identifiable either from the data alone or with the aid of any other information in the data user's possession. Personal data includes any expression of opinion about the individual, but not any expression of intention the data user may have in respect of him.

A 'data subject' is an individual who is the subject of personal data. The Act introduces a new concept of 'sensitive personnel data'. This is data concerning:

- racial or ethnic origins of the data subject
- his political opinions
- religious beliefs or beliefs of a similar nature
- whether he is a member of a trade union
- physical or mental health or condition
- his sexual life
- the commission or alleged commission by him of any offence
- any proceedings for any offence committed or alleged to have been committed by him, the disposal of such proceedings or the sentence of the court in any such proceedings.

16A.2 Data protection principles

The Act lays down eight data protection principles. These are not all the same as the eight data protection principles in the 1984 Act, although there are similarities.

The Act provides interpretation for the application of those principles. The principles are these:

(a) The information contained in personal data must be obtained, and the personal data processed, fairly and lawfully. This principle also stipulates that personal data shall not be processed unless

    (i)   at least one of the following conditions has been met:

- the data subject has consented to it; or
- the processing is **necessary** for one of the following reasons:
  - for the performance of a contract to which the data subject is a party
  - to take steps at the request of the data subject with a view to entering into a contract
  - for the data controller to comply with a legal obligation – other than a contractual obligation – on him
  - to protect the vital interests of the data subject
  - to comply with various public duties
  - for the legitimate interests of the data controller or a third party to whom they are disclosed, except where processing is not warranted in the particular case because of the prejudice to the rights and legitimate freedoms or interests of the data subject (the Secretary of State can specify circumstances in which this condition is, or is not, to be taken to be satisfied).

    (ii) Where the data in question is 'sensitive personnel data' (see 16A.1 above) one of the following conditions must also be met:

- the data subject has given explicit consent to the processing of the data
- the processing is necessary for exercising any right conferred or performing any obligation imposed by law on the data controller in connection with employment
- the processing is necessary to protect the vital interests of the data subject or another in a case where the data controller
  - cannot, or cannot reasonably, be expected to obtain the data subject's consent; or
  - where the data subject has unreasonably withheld his consent
- the data concerns members of a non-profit-making body or trade union and is processed for internal use in a way which protects the data subject's rights and freedoms
- the information has been made public as a result of steps deliberately taken by the data subject
- the processing is necessary
  - for the purposes of or in connection with any legal proceedings or prospective legal proceedings
  - for obtaining legal advice
  - for the purpose otherwise of establishing, exercising or defending legal rights
- the processing is necessary to fulfil one of a number of public functions

- the processing is necessary for medical purposes and is carried out by someone owing a duty of confidentiality equivalent to that of a health professional
- the processing is of information regarding racial or ethnic origins which is carried out with appropriate safeguards for data subjects, where the purpose is to monitor equal opportunities between those of different racial or ethnic origins with a view to promoting equality.

In terms of interpreting the first data protection principle, the Act says that in deciding whether data was obtained fairly and lawfully, the purpose for which it was obtained and used, and questions as to whether any person who provided the information was deceived or misled as to that purpose, must be taken into account.

(b) Personal data is to be held for only one or more specified and lawful purposes and is not to be used or disclosed in a manner incompatible with the specified purpose/s.

(c) Personal data must be adequate, relevant and not excessive in relation to the purposes for which it is held.

(d) Personal data must be accurate and updated if necessary.

(e) Personal data must not be kept for longer than is necessary to fulfil the purpose for which it is held. (This principle is subject to an exception where data is used for historical, statistical or research purposes. In such cases, provided the data subject is not likely to suffer any damage or distress thereby, the data may be kept indefinitely.)

(f) Personal data is to be processed in accordance with the rights of data subjects under the Act.

(g) Appropriate technical and organisational measures must be taken against unauthorised or unlawful processing of personal data and against accidental loss or destruction of or damage to personal data. (In considering whether this principle has been complied with, the state of technological development, the cost of any security measures and the damage that might result from any failure to take those measures have to be balanced against harm that might result from a breach. The organisational measures include assessment of the reliability of staff having access to the personal data.)

(h) Personal data must not be transferred outside the European Economic Area (EEA) unless the place to which it is transferred ensures adequate protection for the rights and freedoms of data sheets in relation to the processing of personal data. (There are certain exemptions from this provision – most important, for these purposes, is where the data subject consents to the transfer of information.)

16A.3 Registration of data controllers

The Act provides for the establishment of a Data Protection Commissioner who replaces the erstwhile position of Data Protection Registrar. All data controllers (with few exceptions) must register with the Commissioner, and must furnish him with:

- their name and address or the name of their nominated representative
- a description of the data being processed or to be processed and the categories of subject to which it relates
- a description of any recipients to whom the data controller intends or may wish to disclose the data
- the name and description of any countries or territories outside the EEA to which he intends or may wish directly or indirectly to transfer the data (ie to help enforce the data protection legislation which restricts personal data from being sent to countries outside the EEA where there is no similar protection)
- a statement where the personal data is of a type which is exempt from the notification requirements and where the notification does not extend to such data. (Personal data is exempt from the registration requirements where it consists only of paper files or health records. In such cases, under transitional arrangements, there is no need to register such data until 24 October 2001 or until the end of any current registration period, if earlier. Where paper records have not been processed since before 28 October 1998 registration is not required for those records until 24 October 2007. Some parts of the Act do, however, apply to such records.)

For those who are already registered under the 1984 Act, their registration continues for the time being.

16A.4 Supervision

The Commissioner has some powers to refuse applications for registration, and orders may be made preventing data from being taken out of the UK. Enforcement notices may also be issued where any person appears to be in breach of the data protection principles.

A Data Protection Tribunal is established to hear appeals from any refusal by the Commissioner of an application for registration or alteration of registered particulars and from any order made by the Commissioner.

16A.5 Individual rights

(a) If the data subject makes a request in writing (including a request in electronic form) he is entitled:
  (i) to be told by the data controller whether he or someone on his behalf is processing that individual's personal data
  (ii) where the data controller acknowledges that he does hold personal data, to be given
    - a description of the personal data
    - the purposes for which it is being processed; and
    - a description of those to whom it is or may be disclosed
    - a copy in permanent form except where:
      - the supply of a copy is not possible;
      - to supply a copy would cause disproportionate effort;
      - the data subject agrees otherwise; or

- the disclosure of the data would disclose information relating to another individual *unless*
  - the other individual has consented to the disclosure of that information; or
  - it would be reasonable in all the circumstances to disclose that information without the consent of that other individual – whether or not this is the case will depend on
    - any duty of confidentiality owed to the other individual
    - any steps taken by the data controller to seek the consent of the other individual
    - whether or not the other individual is capable of giving consent; and
    - any express refusal of his consent by the other individual.
- any necessary explanation to make intelligible information given to the data subject that is unintelligible without explanation
- an explanation of the logic involved in the decision-taking process in relation to data that is or is likely to be the sole basis on which a decision has to be taken that significantly affects the data subject, unless that logic is itself a trade secret
- any information as to the source of that data
  - Where the data comes from another identifiable individual, however, the source can be identified only if the other individual has consented or if it would be reasonable in all the circumstances to disclose that information without the consent of the other individual (see above).

(b) An individual is entitled to serve a data controller with a written 'data subject notice' requiring the data controller to cease or not to begin processing (or processing for a specified purpose or in a specified manner) personal data regarding that individual. This can be done only where the processing is causing or is likely to cause unwarranted and substantial distress to the data subject or another. This right is unavailable if the individual has, *inter alia*, given his consent to the processing. It will therefore be important, having regard to the wide way in which 'processing' is defined under the Act, for employers to obtain the consent of their employees that they may process any personal information in such ways as may be deemed necessary.

(c) An individual is entitled to serve a notice on the data controller requiring that no decision which significantly affects him be taken based solely on a system which automatically processes their personal data. Examples given by the Act include the data subject's performance at work. Presumably this would also include computerised attendance records and other more esoteric software that may be used for career and manpower planning purposes.

The data controller must reply to the data subject within 21 days telling him what steps he intends to take to comply with the data subject notice.

(d) A person who suffers damages or distress as a result of any breach of the Act can be awarded compensation against the data controller unless the data controller can prove that he took such care as was reasonable in the circumstances to comply with the requirement.

(e) A data subject can also apply to the court for an order requiring a data controller to rectify, block erase or destroy inaccurate information and any expression of opinion based on inaccurate information.

16A.6 Exemptions

The following data are totally exempt from the provisions of the Act:

(a) data held for purposes of safeguarding national security

(b) certain data concerned with crime and taxation

(c) since the facility for data subjects to have access to data now encompasses medical reports, there are provisions under which the Secretary of State can introduce exemptions from the subject access provisions of the Act in respect of matters concerning, *inter alia*, the mental and physical health or condition of the data subject. No such provisions have yet been brought into force; however, it seems likely that such provisions will be made at least to reflect the erstwhile restrictions on subject access that were contained in the Access to Health Records Act 1990. These allowed disclosure to be refused where it might cause serious harm to any individual.

(d) data held by unincorporated clubs regarding their members

(e) data which is required by law to be publicly available

(f) data held by an individual for domestic or recreational purposes.

17   Deregulation and Contracting Out Act 1994

Amends the Employment Agencies Act 1973, Betting Gaming and Lotteries Act 1963 and Shops Act 1950.

Is in part repealed by and consolidated into the Employment Rights Act 1996.

17.1   Employment agencies

(a) Removes the requirement for employment agencies and employment businesses to be licensed

(b) Prohibition Orders

   (i) The Act introduces a system through which an employment tribunal can, on the application of the Secretary of State, make an order either:
   - prohibiting an individual from being involved in an employment agency or business; or
   - imposing conditions on their involvement.

   (ii) Before making any such order the tribunal must be satisfied that the individual was responsible, or partly responsible, for the improper conduct of the business. Where there is more than one person who manages the business all are equally responsible for any misconduct of the business unless they can show that it happened without their connivance or consent and without negligence on their part.

(iii) A prohibition or condition imposed by an employment tribunal can last for a period of up to 10 years.

(iv) A person on whom an order is made can apply to have the order varied or can appeal to the EAT against the tribunal's decision (on a point of law only).

(v) Failure to comply with a Prohibition Order is dealt with by criminal law sanctions.

17.2   Sunday working

Betting shop workers were given similar rights to those given to other shop workers under the Sunday Trading Act 1994 (the provisions for both betting shop and other shop workers are now consolidated into the Employment Rights Act 1996 *qv*). (See 36.5.)

Ss 17 and 22 of the Shops Act 1950 are both repealed. These sections

* gave shop workers time off in lieu for Sunday working; and
* restricted shop workers from having to work more than three Sundays in any month.

17A   Deregulation (Deduction from Pay of Union Subscriptions) Order 1998 (SI 1998 No. 1529)

Amends Trade Union and Labour Relations (Consolidation) Act 1992

Removes the rather cumbersome machinery instituted by TURERA in relation to the check-off system. The amendments have been inserted into the relevant section of the Trade Union and Labour Relations (Consolidation) Act 1992 (see 102.9 below)

18   Disabled Persons (Employment) Acts 1944 and 1958

Are largely repealed and replaced, for employment purposes, by the Disability Discrimination Act 1995 (*qv*).

19   Disability Discrimination Act 1995

Repeals much of the Disabled Persons (Employment) Act 1944 and amends Disabled Persons (Employment) Act 1958, Chronically Sick and Disabled Persons Act 1970, Employment Protection (Consolidation) Act 1978, Local Government and Housing Act 1989, Education Act 1993. Amended by Disability Rights Commission Act 1999 and Disability Discrimination (Exemption for Small Employers) Order 1998, Disability Discrimination Act 1995, Employment Rights (Disputes Resolutions) Act 1998.

19.1   Disability

A person who has a physical or mental impairment which has a long-term and substantial adverse effect on his ability to carry out normal day-to-day activities has a disability for purposes of the Act. It should be remembered that the rights under the Act affect people with disabilities individually so that if a person with one leg is discriminated against by being refused a job because of his disability, it is no defence for an employer to have hired a person with one arm to do that job.

1   'Impairment'

(a) There is no general definition of what an impairment is.

(b) A mental impairment amounts to a disability only if it results from an illness which is clinically well recognised.

(c) Specific conditions may be declared by regulations to be or not to be impairments for purposes of the Act. The Disability Discrimination (Meaning of Disability) Regulations 1996 (SI 1996 No. 1455) specify certain matters as not being impairments:

- addictions – unless they originally arose from medically prescribed drugs
- tendencies to setting fires, stealing, physical or sexual abuse, exhibitionism or voyeurism
- hay fever – although this can be taken into account where its effects aggravate another impairment
- tattoos and body piercing that have been done for non-medical purposes.

2   'Substantial adverse effect'

(a) There is no definition of what amounts to a 'substantial adverse effect'.

(b) Regulations can prescribe that a particular kind of effect on the ability of a person to perform normal day-to-day activities shall or shall not be considered to be 'substantial'.

(c) Severe disfigurement

(i)   An impairment which consists of severe disfigurement is to be treated as having a long-term substantial adverse effect on a person's ability to carry out normal day-to-day activities.

(ii) Cases where severe disfigurement is not to be treated as having that effect may be prescribed by Regulations. Tattoos and voluntary body piercing have already been proscribed for these purposes (see Disability Discrimination (Meaning of Disability) Regulations 1996 (SI 1996 No. 1455)).

(d) Impact of medical treatment

Where an impairment would be likely to have a substantial adverse effect on a person but for the fact that measures are being taken to correct or to treat it, the impairment is nonetheless treated as having a substantial adverse effect.

(i)   'Measures' include medical treatment and the use of prostheses or other aids.

(ii) This does not apply to people whose eyesight is correctable by glasses or contact lenses.

(iii) Regulations can be made to exclude other cases where a person receiving treatment or subject to other measures is not to be considered substantially adversely affected by the impairment in question.

3   Long-term effect
(a) An impairment is considered to have a long-term effect if:
    (i)   it has lasted 12 months or more
    (ii)   it is likely to last for at least 12 months; or
    (iii) it is likely to last for the rest of that person's life.
(b) Guidance may be issued by the Secretary of State (which must be taken into account by any court or tribunal, where it is relevant) as to whether any impairment may or may not be considered as having a long-term effect.
(c) Recurrence
    (i)   If the condition ceases to have a substantial adverse effect on the person's ability to carry out normal day-to-day activities but the effect is expected to recur then it is to be treated as continuing to have that effect.
    (ii)   Regulations can prescribe
        ● when the threat of recurrence is to be ignored for these purposes; and
        ● circumstances where an effect that would not otherwise be considered long-term is to be considered to be long-term and vice versa.
4   Normal day-to-day activities
(a) The impairment must affect one or more of the following if it is to affect 'normal day-to-day activities':
    (i)   mobility
    (ii)   manual dexterity
    (iii) physical co-ordination
    (iv)   continence
    (v)   ability to lift, carry or otherwise move day-to-day objects
    (vi)   speech, hearing or eyesight
    (vii) memory or ability to concentrate, learn or understand; or
    (viii) perception of the risk of physical danger.
(b) Regulations may prescribe where an impairment does or does not have any of the above effects or where it is to be taken as not affecting the person's ability to carry out normal day-to-day activities.
5   Deemed disability
(a) Registered disabled: A person who was registered as disabled on 12 January 1995 is to be taken to be disabled for three years from that date and is thereafter treated as having been disabled during that period. Under the new provisions disabled people are no longer registered as such.
(b) Progressive conditions: A person who is suffering from a progressive condition which is likely to result in his having a substantial impairment is to be treated as having a substantial impairment (examples of such conditions include cancer, MS, muscular dystrophy, and HIV infection).
(c) Past disabilities: The Act applies to those with past disabilities, and, with some modifications, applies to those who are currently disabled.

19.2 Small employers

None of the duties under the Act apply to employers with fewer than 15 employees. (The original 'small employers' exemption applied where the employer employed fewer than 20 employees. This number was reduced by Disability Discrimination (Exemption for Small Employers) Order 1998 (SI 1998 No. 2618) to its current level of 15. The maximum number of employees an employer may have while being considered a 'small employer' under the Act may be reduced by the Secretary of State by Order.)

19.3   Discrimination by employers

1   It is unlawful for an employer to discriminate against a disabled person (in relation to employment at an establishment in Great Britain):
(a) at the pre-employment stage:
    (i)   in the arrangements he makes for determining who should be offered that employment
    (ii)   in the terms on which he offers that employment
    (iii) by refusing to offer, or deliberately not offering him, that employment; and
(b) against a disabled employee of his:
    (i)   in the terms of employment that he offers
    (ii)   in the opportunities that he affords him for
- promotion
- transfer
- training; or
- receiving any other benefit.
  - 'Benefits' include facilities or services.
  - This does not apply where the employer is concerned with the provision of benefits of that description to the public (whether or not for payment) or to a section of the public which includes the employee unless:
    - what is provided to the public is materially different from what is provided to his employees; or
    - the provision of the benefit in question is regulated by the employee's contract of employment; or
    - the benefits relate to training (s 4(3)).

    (iii) by refusing/failing to afford him any of the above opportunities
(c) by dismissing the employee or subjecting him to any other detriment.
2   'Employment'
As with the sex and race discrimination legislation, 'employment' is widely defined. It means employment under a contract of apprenticeship or employment or under a contract personally to do any work. As such, it includes those who are self-employed and who are working through employment agencies provided they are hired to do the work personally.
3   'Discrimination'
(a) An employer discriminates against a disabled person if for a reason related to that disability (NB this is concerned with the individual's particular disability, not with the fact that the person is disabled in general terms):

- he treats him less favourably than he treats or would treat others to whom that reason does not or would not apply; and
- he cannot show that the treatment in question is justified.

(i) 'Justification'

Treatment is 'justified' only if the reason for it:

- is material to the circumstances of the particular case; and
- is substantial.

Regulations can be made to provide when any treatment is and is not to be taken to be justified. Such regulations may make provision

- by reference to the cost of providing any benefit; and
- in relation to benefits under an occupational pension scheme with a view to enabling uniform rates of contributions to be maintained (see Disability Discrimination (Employment) Regulations 1996 (SI 1996 No. 1456)).

Where an employer has failed to comply with the duty to make reasonable adjustments to accommodate a disabled person (see 19.4 below), then any question of whether or not the employer was justified in any discrimination against that person has to be approached as if the employer had made all reasonable adjustments that were necessary. Or, put another way, the employer cannot rely on his failure to make reasonable adjustments as justification for discriminating on grounds of disability.

(ii) NB Apart from the requirement to make reasonable adjustments (see 19.4 below), the Act, insofar as it deals with discrimination in the employment field, does not require an employer to give a disabled person better treatment than he would give to any other person.

(b) An employer also discriminates against a disabled person if:

(i) he fails to comply with any duty to make reasonable adjustments (see 19.4); and

(ii) he cannot show that his failure to comply with the duty in question is justified (for 'justification', see 19.3.3(a) above).

19.4 Employer's duty to make adjustments

1   The duty to make adjustments is enshrined in s 6 of the Act:

(b) Where

(i) arrangements made by or on behalf of an employer; or

(ii) any physical feature of premises occupied by the employer

place the disabled person concerned at a substantial disadvantage by comparison to people who are not disabled, the employer is under a duty to take such steps as it is reasonable for him to take in all the circumstances of the case, to prevent the arrangements or feature from having that effect.

(b) Regulations can be made

(i) to say what are and are not physical features for these purposes (see Reg. 9 Disability Discrimination (Employment) Regulations 1996 (SI 1996 No. 1456))

(ii) to say when certain arrangements or physical features are and are not to be taken to cause substantial disadvantage to disabled people; and

(iii) to add to the duties imposed by s 6.

2 General limitations on the duty under s 6:

(a) The duty to make adjustments under s 6 does not apply to:

(i) any benefit under an occupational pension scheme; or

(ii) any benefit payable in money or monies worth under a scheme or arrangement for the benefit of employees in respect of:

- termination of service
- retirement, old age or death
- accident, injury, sickness or invalidity
- any other prescribed matter (see the Disability Discrimination (Employment) Regulations 1996 (SI 1996 No. 1456)).

(b) The duty applies only for purposes of determining whether or not an employer has discriminated against a disabled person and a breach of this duty is not therefore actionable otherwise than within the terms of the DDA.

3 'The disabled person concerned' for purposes of s 6 is:

(a) in the case of discriminatory arrangements for determining to whom employment should be offered any disabled person:

(i) who is a job applicant; or

(ii) who has notified the employer that he might be an applicant for the job; or

(b) in any other case a person who is:

(i) an applicant for the job; or

(ii) an employee.

4 Reasonable steps:

(a) The requirement for an employer to take reasonable steps to prevent any arrangements he has made (as opposed to physical features) from having the effect of placing a disabled person at a substantial disadvantage does not apply to:

(i) dismissal, or

(ii) subjecting the person to any other detriment.

At first glance this might seem to mean that an employer is under no duty, for example, to change a redundancy policy which has the effect of selecting disabled people for redundancy before able-bodied people. Any such discrimination would, however, be subject to the general requirement not to discriminate against the disabled person in question by dismissing him or subjecting him to a detriment. (A detriment might occur in this type of case if, for example, the employee was moved to another, less desirable job, rather than being dismissed in the redundancy situation.)

(b) The type of steps that it may be reasonable for an employer to take to obviate the adverse impact of any discriminatory effect are exemplified by the Act itself. These include:

(i) making adjustments to premises

(ii)   allocating some of the disabled person's duties to another person

(iii) transferring the disabled person to fill an existing vacancy

(iv) altering his hours of work

(v)   assigning him to a different place of work

(vi) allowing him to be absent during working hours for rehabilitation, assessment or treatment

(vii) giving him or arranging for him to be given training

(viii) acquiring or modifying equipment for his use

(ix) modifying instructions or reference manuals

(x)   modifying procedures for the testing or assessment of the disabled person

(xi) providing a reader or interpreter

(xii) providing supervision.

However, these are only examples and the steps which it may be reasonable for an employer to take will depend on the circumstances. For example, in the case of a job applicant it would normally be reasonable to hold the interviews in a place that is accessible to the candidate and at a time that does not prevent him, because of his disability, from attending the interview.

(c) In determining whether it is reasonable for an employer to have to take a particular step in order to prevent a disabled person being put at a substantial disadvantage as compared with a person who is not disabled, the following must be considered:

(i)   the extent to which the step would prevent the effect in question

(ii)   the extent to which it is practicable for the employer to take the step

(iii) the financial and other costs that would be incurred by the employer in taking the step and the extent to which taking it would disrupt his activities

(iv) the extent of the employer's financial and other resources

(v)   the availability to the employer of financial or other assistance with respect to taking the step.

(d) Regulations may

(i)   define prescribed steps which it is and is not reasonable to take; and

(ii)   the circumstances in which it is or is not reasonable for an employer to have to take those steps.

(iii) These regulations may make provisions by reference to the cost of taking any such measures.

5 Limitation on the duty to take steps

An employer has no duty to take steps if the employer did not know and could not reasonably be expected to know that a person who is or may be an applicant for employment is in fact a disabled applicant or potential applicant for employment.

19.5 Victimisation

1   A person victimises another if he treats that other less favourably because he has:

(a) brought proceedings against any person under the DDA
(b) given evidence or information in connection with any such proceedings
(c) otherwise done anything under the DDA in relation to any person
(d) alleged that anyone has contravened the DDA.
2   A person victimises another if he treats that other less favourably because he believes or suspects that the other has done or intends to do any of the things set out in 19.5.1.
3   A person cannot claim victimisation if he has made a false allegation.

19.6   Enforcement

1   Enforcement in the employment field is through the tribunal system. A case must be brought within three months of the discrimination complained of. As with sex and race discrimination claims, the tribunal can extend time for presenting a complaint if it considers that it is just and equitable to do so in the circumstances of the case.
2   Where a tribunal finds that a complaint is well founded, it can:
(a) make a declaration as to the applicant's and the employer's rights in relation to the matters complained of
(b) order the employer to pay compensation (the compensation in these cases, as with sex and race discrimination, is without limit and can include damages for injury to feelings caused by the discrimination)
(c) recommend that the employer takes such action as the tribunal considers reasonable to obviate or reduce the adverse effect on the applicant of the matter complained of. The tribunal can also specify the time within which such action must be taken. If the employer fails to take the recommended action then the tribunal can award additional compensation.

DfEE Code of Practice 1996

In 1996 the DfEE produced a Code of Practice for the elimination of discrimination in the field of employment against disabled persons or persons who have had a disability. The Code is not legally binding in its own right, but its provisions are admissible in evidence before a tribunal or a court. The Code, as well as going through the law on disabilities and employment and giving helpful examples of the provisions of the DDA, makes a few fundamental suggestions which employers should take into account:
1   Do not make assumptions – talk to the individual disabled person to see what the effects of his disability might be. In most cases he will have a better idea than you as to what his limitations are and how any limitations can be got round.
2   Consider if expert advice is needed – while there is no obligation to get expert advice, it may be helpful to do so, especially where the person is newly disabled and therefore less likely to know what his limitations (if any) will be due to the disability.

3 Plan ahead – where changes are being made in buildings, etc. consider the possible effect on potential disabled job applicants.

4 Promote equal opportunities – employers who have equal opportunities policies are likely, says the Code, to have that counted in their favour by a court or tribunal.

It should be borne in mind, in the context of promoting equal opportunities, that:

(a) the duty to disabled people is owed to them as individuals rather than as a class; and

(b) there is no prohibition on positive discrimination in favour of the disabled – provided that there is no discrimination as between people with different disabilities. (NB There are provisions that do allow for discrimination between people with different types of disabilities, but these are limited broadly to charities which are set up to deal with particular types of disability.)

Employers needing specialist help regarding the employment of people with disabilities should contact their local Placing, Assessment and Counselling Team (PACT). PACTs are part of the Employment Service.

19A Disability Discrimination (Exemption for Small Employers) Order 1998 SI 1998 No 2618

Amends the Disability Discrimination Act 1995

Reduces from 20 to 15 the maximum number of employees who can be employed if the employer is to be entitled to claim exemption from the Disability Discrimination Act 1995.

19B Disability Rights Commission Act 1999

Amends the Disability Discrimination Act 1995

It is currently proposed to set up the Disability Rights Commission (DRC) in Spring 2000. The DRC's main duties will be similar to those of the EOC and the CRE in relation to sex and race discrimination respectively, ie:

- to work towards the elimination of discrimination against disabled people;
- to provide assistance for disabled people;
- to promote equal opportunities for the disabled;
- to provide a central source of information and advice to key sets of people including disabled people and employers;
- to encourage good practice in the treatment of the disabled;
- to advise the government on the operation of the Disability Discrimination Act 1995.
- to prepare and review statutory codes of practice; and
- to undertake formal investigations.

20 Dock Work Act 1989

(a) Abolished the Dock Workers Employment Scheme and the National Dock Labour Board.

(b) Makes provisions for redundancy payments for dock workers who are made redundant and provides that those registered as dock workers at the date that the Act was passed are to have their previous service while registered counted towards their period of continuous employment.

21 Education Acts 1944 to 1973 (largely repealed by Education Act 1996)

22 Education Act 1993 (repealed by Education Act 1996)

22A Education Act 1996

Consolidates and repeals much of the earlier Education legislation. Repeals Education Acts 1944, 1946, 1959, 1964, 1968, 1975, 1976, 1979 1981, 1993, Education (Work Experience) Act 1973 and the Education (School-leaving Dates) Act 1976.

Amends Children and Young Persons Act 1963, Education Act 1962, 1967, 1973, 1980 and 1994, Employment Act 1990, Disability Discrimination Act 1995, Employment Rights Act 1996, Sex Discrimination Act 1975 and Race Relations Act 1976.

Amended by Education Act 1997.

1   *Compulsory school age*

The Act sets down when a person is of compulsory school age. A person ceases to be of compulsory school age if he attains the age of 16:

(a) on the school-leaving date for that year; or

(b) after the school-leaving date for that year, but before the beginning of the following school year;

otherwise the end of compulsory school age will be the school-leaving date which immediately follows his 16th birthday.

2   *Employment of children*

(a) Any individual who is not over compulsory school age is a 'child' for purposes of statute

(b) The Act gives the local education authority certain powers to oversee the employment of children in local authority education:

   (i)   The authority can require a parent or employer to provide it with information so that the authority can determine whether the child is being employed in a manner which renders him unfit to obtain the full benefit of his education.

   (ii) If it appears to the authority that the child is being employed in such a manner, it can serve a notice on the employer:

     ● prohibiting him from employing the child; or

     ● imposing any restrictions on the child's employment that the authority considers expedient.

   (iii) An employer who fails to comply with any prohibition or restrictions imposed by a local education authority is liable to prosecution.

(iv)   The local education authority is given powers of entry to enforce any restrictions or prohibitions it may have imposed on an employer.

3   *Work experience in last year of compulsory schooling*

During the last year of compulsory schooling the local education authority or the governing body of a grant maintained school can make arrangements to provide children with work experience as part of their education

22B   Education Act 1997

Amends the Education Act 1996 alters the definition of compulsory school age, but only in respect of when it begins.

23   Education (Work Experience) Act 1973 (repealed by Education Act 1996)

24   Employers' Liability (Compulsory Insurance) Act 1969

Amended by Police Act 1997.

Prescribes that all employers must insure against liability for personal injury and disease sustained by their employees and arising out of, or in the course of, their employment in Great Britain.

25   Employers' Liability (Defective Equipment) Act 1969

Amended by Police Act 1997.

Makes an employer liable, without proof of fault on his part, in all cases where an employee sustains personal injury in the course of his employment 'in consequence of a defect in equipment provided by his employer for the purposes of the employer's business'.

26   Employment Acts 1980 to 1988 and 1990

Largely repealed and consolidated by TULRA.

27   Employment Act 1989

Amended by Employment Act 1990, Further and Higher Education Act 1992 and Education Act 1993.

Amends Employment of Women, Young Persons and Children Act 1920, Shops Act 1950, Factories Act 1961, Children and Young Persons Act 1963, Employment and Training Act 1973, Health and Safety at Work etc. Act 1974, Employment Protection Act 1975, Social Security Act 1975, Sex Discrimination Acts 1975 and 1986, Race Relations Act 1976, Employment Protection (Consolidation) Act 1978, Employment and Training Act 1981, Agricultural Training Board Act 1982, Industrial Training Act 1982, Employment Act 1988. Repeals Young Persons (Employment) Acts 1938 and 1964.

27.1   Sex discrimination law amendments

Unusually for an 'Employment Act', the 1989 Act is primarily concerned with updating the Sex Discrimination Act 1975 to bring it into line with the European Directive on sex discrimination.

(a) Removing the effects of discriminatory legislation passed before the Sex Discrimination Act 1975

Where any provision of an Act which was passed before the Sex Discrimination Act 1975 imposes a requirement to do anything which would be discriminatory under the SDA 1975, then that provision is 'of no effect'. This provision extends to cover post-1975 re-enactments of pre-1975 Acts and also includes any statutory instrument made under any such Act – whether the statutory instrument was made before or after the 1975 Act was passed.

The Secretary of State for Employment is also given power to amend, revoke or repeal any such provision of any such Act or of any statutory instrument made under any such Act.

(b) Circumstances in which discrimination is permissible

The Act provides that discrimination against women is not unlawful insofar as it is necessary:

 (i) to comply with any existing (ie pre-SDA 1975) statutory provision (or any statutory instrument passed under any such statute) concerning the protection of women in relation to pregnancy, maternity, or risks specifically affecting women; or

 (ii) to comply with the requirement to take care of the health and safety of women in relation to pregnancy, maternity, or risks specifically affecting women.

(c) Exemptions from the provisions of the SDA 1975

 (i) Employment as a head teacher or principal of an educational establishment where any instrument relating to the establishment requires that its head be of a particular religious order

 (ii) Employment as the head, a fellow or any other member of the academic staff of any college or similar institution where any instrument relating to the establishment requires that the position in question be filled by a woman.

(d) Discrimination as regards training

 (i) Section 14 of the Sex Discrimination Act 1975, which was concerned with the provision of training by vocational training bodies, is re-enacted with amendments (the equivalent provision of the Race Relations Act 1976 is similarly amended).

 (ii) The Secretary of State is empowered to allow for discrimination in favour of single parents in relation to certain types of training.

27.2 Removal of restrictions on hours of work, etc. in respect of women and young persons

Most of the restrictions on the hours of employment for women and young persons are lifted. This legislation does not, however, affect the restrictions on the employment of 'children' (ie those under minimum school-leaving age).

27.3 Race discrimination

(a) Discrimination as regards training

Section 13 of the Race Relations Act 1976, which was concerned with the provision of training by vocational training bodies, is re-enacted with amendments (the equivalent provision of the Sex Discrimination Act 1975 is similarly amended).

(b) Safety helmets

A Sikh who is wearing a turban is exempted from any legal requirement to wear a safety helmet on a construction site. If he is injured, however, then any liability on the person causing the injury is limited to the damage that would have been done if the employee had been wearing a safety helmet.

28 Employment Agencies Act 1973

Amended by Employment Protection Act 1975, Deregulation and Contracting Out Act 1994, Police Act 1997.

Lays down rules for running employment agencies and employment businesses. The former requirement for employment agencies to be licensed was removed by the Deregulation and Contracting Out Act 1994.

29 Employment and Training Act 1973

Amended by Employment Protection Act 1975, Employment and Training Act 1981, Agricultural Training Board Act 1982, Industrial Training Act 1982 and Employment Acts 1988 and 1989.

The Manpower Services Commission (MSC) is established as an independent body to run the public employment and training services. The two executive arms of the MSC set up by this Act have now been disbanded.

30 Employment (Continental Shelf) Act 1978

Amended by Trade Union and Labour Relations (Consolidation) Act 1992.

The Oil and Gas (Enterprise) Act 1982 contains provisions repealing the following extensions of the sex and race discrimination legislation. An Order will need to be made under the 1982 Act to give effect to these repeals.

The Act extends the rights under the Sex Discrimination Act 1975 and Race Relations Act 1976 to those working on 'cross-boundary' oil fields in the North Sea. A 'cross-boundary' oil field is one that is partly inside and partly outside United Kingdom territorial waters.

31 Employment Medical Advisory Services Act 1972

Amends Factories Act 1961.

Sets up the Employment Medical Advisory Service (EMAS). Allows an EMAS medical adviser to serve notice on a factory occupier requiring the occupier to allow for medical examination of employees in factories where the medical adviser is of the opinion that an employee's health has been, is being or may be injured by reason of the work he is being, or may be, called upon to do. Provides for EMAS medical advisers to take over medical examinations required by the Factories Act 1961. Payment for these services is made to the Secretary of State.

32   Employment of Children Act 1973 (relevant parts subsumed into Education Act 1996)

Amends Children and Young Persons Act 1933.

33   Employment of Women, Young Persons and Children Act 1920

Amended by Employment of Women, Young Persons and Children Act 1936 and Employment Act 1989.

Restricts employment of children in industrial undertakings.

34   Employment Protection Act 1975 (EPA) (repealed)

Largely re-enacted in Employment Protection (Consolidation) Act 1978. Those parts concerning collective matters have now been consolidated into Trade Union and Labour Relations (Consolidation) Act 1992.

35   Employment Protection (Consolidation) Act 1978 (repealed)

Repealed and consolidated into the Employment Rights Act 1996.

35A   Employment Relations Act 1999

Amends Employment Agencies Act 1973, Sex Discrimination Act 1975, Race Relations Act 1976, Trade Union and Labour Relations (Consolidation) Act 1992, Trade Union Reform and Employment Rights Act 1993 Disability Discrimination Act 1995, Employment Rights Act 1996, Employment Tribunals Act 1996, Employment Rights (Dispute Resolution) Act 1998, National Minimum Wage Act 1998, Public Interest Disclosure Act 1998,

Much of this Act consists of 'enabling legislation' which simply allows for the Secretary of State to make Regulations to make law in a particular area; this, for example, is the case with family and domestic leave. Even where the Regulations are not to create the law, they are still required to give effect to the provisions of the Act. At the time of writing few of the necessary Regulations needed to bring the provisions of the Act into being have been made. The following substantive provisions have been brought in:

(a) *Reduction in effect of exclusion clauses in fixed-term contracts*

Employees on fixed-term contracts of a year or more with exclusion clauses from claiming unfair dismissal are, nonetheless allowed to present an unfair dismissal claim if they are dismissed on or after 30 September 1999 because of:
  ● pregnancy or childbirth; or
  ● assertion of a statutory right.

The facility to exclude the right to bring an unfair dismissal claim in a fixed-term contract of one year or more is removed:

LIVERPOOL JOHN MOORES UNIVERSITY
LEARNING SERVICES

- for all fixed-term contracts entered into after 25 October 1999; or
- where a fixed-term contract is renewed after 25 October 1999; or
- where the agreement to waive unfair dismissal rights is entered into after that date.

(b) *Trade union matters*
- Right not to be subjected to a detriment on grounds of trade union activities or membership redefined
  - The right not to have action short of dismissal taken on grounds of trade union activities or membership is changed to a right not to be subjected to a detriment on grounds of trade union activities or membership. This makes the protection equivalent to that afforded under the sex and race discrimination legislation.
- Commissioner for the Rights of Trade Union Members and Commissioner for Protection Against Unlawful Industrial Action
  - Both of these posts are abolished.
  - The duties of the Certification Officer are, however, widened to encompass some of the functions of the Commissioner for the Rights of Trade Union Members in practice.
- The duties of the Certification Officer are considerably extended by the Act

(c) *Changes in unfair dismissal awards*
The maximum compensatory award for unfair dismissal is raised to £50,000.
The upper limit of for unfair dismissal compensation does not apply where the dismissal is for a health and safety reason or because of a protected disclosure.
The maximum amount of a 'week's pay' for calculation of an employee's basic award for unfair dismissal and redundancy payment entitlement, the maximum daily amount of a guarantee payment and the new upper limit for the unfair dismissal compensatory award are all index-linked from October 1999.

(d) *National Minimum Wage for those in religious communities*
From 25 October 1999 those who are members of residential religious communities are excluded from the right to receive the National Minimum Wage.

36 Employment Rights Act 1996

Repeals and consolidates in part or in whole *inter alia*: Betting, Gaming and Lotteries Act 1963, Race Relations Act 1976, Employment Protection (Consolidation) Act 1978, Education Act 1980, Employment Act 1980, Magistrates' Courts Act 1980, Finance Act 1980, New Towns Act 1981, Civil Aviation Act 1982, Oil and Gas Enterprise Act 1982, Social Security and Housing Benefits Act 1982, Employment Act 1982, Water Act 1983, Reserve Forces (Safeguard of Employment) Act 1985, Local Government Act 1985, Insolvency Act 1985, Housing (Consequential Provisions) Act 1986, Insolvency Act 1986, Wages Act 1986, Social Security Act 1986, Sex Discrimination Act 1986, Income and Corporation Taxes Act 1988, Norfolk and Suffolk Broads Act 1988, Legal Aid Act 1988, Education Reform Act 1988, Housing Act 1988, Dock Work Act 1989, Water Act 1989, Electricity Act 1989, Employment Act 1989, National Health Service and Community Care Act

1990, Employment Act 1990, Environmental Protection Act 1990, Social Security (Consequential Provisions) Act 1992, Further and Higher Education Act 1992, Trade Union and Labour Relations (Consolidation) Act 1992, Trade Union Reform and Employment Rights Act 1993, Pension Schemes Act 1993, Race Relations (Remedies) Act 1994, Social Security (Incapacity for Work) Act 1994, Sunday Trading Act 1994, Deregulation and Contracting Out Act 1994, Health Authorities Act 1995, Environment Act 1995, Pensions Act 1995, Disability Discrimination Act 1995, Reserve Forces Act 1996, Time Off for Public Duties Order 1990, SI 1990/1870, Sex Discrimination and Equal Pay (Remedies) Regulations 1993, SI 1993/2798, Employment Protection (Part-time Employees) Regulations 1995, SI 1995/31, Time Off for Public Duties Order 1995, SI 1995/694, Collective Redundancies and Transfer of Undertakings (Protection of Employment) (Amendment) Regulations 1995, SI 1995/2587, Environment Act 1995 (Consequential Amendments) Regulations 1996, SI 1996/593, Environment Act 1995 (Consequential and Transitional Provisions) (Scotland) Regulations 1996, SI 1996/973.

Amended by Police Act 1997, Police (Health and Safety) Act 1997, Employment Rights (Disputes Resolutions) Act 1998, National Minimum Wage Act 1998, Public Interest Disclosure Act 1998, Teaching and Higher Education Act 1998, Working Time Regulations 1998, Collective Redundancies and Transfer of Undertakings (Protection of Employment) (Amendment) Regulations 1999, Unfair Dismissal and Statement of Reasons for Dismissal (Variation of Qualifying Period) Order 1999.

36.1 Statement of terms and conditions of employment

Originally ss 1 to 7 EPCA (and s 11 re enforcement) as amended by TURERA. Now ss 1–6 ERA (and ss 11 and 12 re enforcement).

(a) *The right*
- (i) An employee is entitled to be given a written statement of the main terms and conditions of employment within two months of beginning employment (the reduction from three months within which to give the statement to two months was brought about by TURERA). If the employee is going to be sent abroad for a period of more than a month within this initial two-month period then the statement must be given before he leaves. The employee is entitled to a statement of terms and conditions if his employment is terminated after he has been employed for more than one but less than two months.
- (ii) Certain of the terms must be included in a single document (these are asterisked in the list in (b) below). The facility, allowed by the EPCA, to refer to other documents for these terms was severely curtailed by TURERA.
- (iii) If there are no particulars to be entered under any particular head in the particulars set out in (b) below then this fact must be specified.

(b) *Particulars to be specified*
- (i) the names of the employer and employee*
- (ii) the date when the employment began*

(iii)   the date on which the employee's period of continuous employment began (taking into account any employment with a previous employer which counts towards that period)*

(iv)   the scale or rate of remuneration or the method of calculating remuneration*

(v)   intervals at which remuneration is paid (ie weekly, monthly or other specified intervals)*

(vi)   any terms and conditions relating to hours of work (including any terms and conditions relating to normal working hours)*

(vii)   any terms and conditions relating to
  • entitlement to holidays, public holidays and holiday pay (the particulars must be sufficient to enable the employee's entitlement, including entitlement to accrued holiday pay on termination of employment, to be calculated)*
  • incapacity for work due to sickness or injury, including any sick pay; and
  • pensions and pension schemes (the requirement to notify this item is excluded in relation to certain pension schemes set up by statute).

(viii) the length of notice required from each party to terminate the employee's employment

(ix)   job title or a brief description of the employee's work* (amended by TURERA – previously only job title was allowed)

(x)   where the employment is not intended to be permanent, the period for which it is expected to continue or, if it is for a fixed term, the date when it is to end (amended by TURERA – previously there was no reference to the period for which a temporary job was expected to last). It should be noted that where the employment is for less than one month then there is no entitlement to a s 1 statement (this was reduced from three months by TURERA)

(xi)   the place of work or, if the employee is required or permitted to work at various places, an indication of that fact and of the employer's address* (introduced by TURERA)

(xii)   any collective agreements which directly affect the terms and conditions of the employment including, where the employer was not a party, the persons by whom they were made (introduced by TURERA)

(xiii) where the employee is required to work outside the UK for more than one month
  • the period for which he is to work outside the United Kingdom
  • the currency in which his remuneration will be paid while working outside the UK
  • any additional remuneration payable/benefits to be provided to or in respect of him, by reason of his being required to work outside the UK; and
  • any terms and conditions relating to his return to the United Kingdom (introduced by TURERA).

(c) *Reference to other documents*
  (i)　The section 1 statement may refer the employee for particulars to do with incapacity for work due to sickness or injury, including sick pay provisions, and for details of pensions and pension schemes to another document that is reasonably accessible to the employee.
  (ii)　The section 1 statement may refer to the law or to the provisions of any collective agreement directly affecting the employee's terms and conditions which is reasonably accessible to the employee, for the length of notice to be given by either party to terminate his employment.
This very limited facility to refer the employee to other documentation, brought in by TURERA, can be contrasted to the original provisions of the EPCA which allowed the employer to refer the employee to other documents for all the items which had to be notified to him under s 1.

(d) *Note of disciplinary procedure and pensions*
A section 1 statement must also include:
  (i)　in relation to discipline and grievance
    ● a note of any disciplinary rules applicable to the employee (the employee can be referred to another document for this)
    ● a note specifying to whom the employee can appeal if he is dissatisfied with any disciplinary decision, and how to appeal
    ● a note specifying to whom the employee can appeal if he has a grievance, and how to deal with this
    ● a note of any further steps available in the grievance or disciplinary procedures
    ● a note relating to discipline and grievance is not required if the employer employs fewer than 20 employees.
  (ii)　a note saying whether there is a contracting-out certificate (under the Pension Schemes Act 1993) in force.

(e) *Statement of changes*
If there are changes in any items of which particulars are required to be given, the employer must give the employee a written statement containing particulars of the change at the earliest opportunity and, in any event, not later than one month after the change in question (or before the employee goes abroad if he is leaving to work outside the UK for more than a month before the statement of changes would otherwise be due).
  Where the employer changes its name or there is a change of employer which does not affect the employee's continuity of employment then that change can be noted in a statement of change rather than supplying a new statement. If a statement of change is given where there is a change of employer then that statement must also give the employee's original continuity date.

(f) *Enforcement*
  (i)　If the employer does not give an employee a section 1 statement or a statement of changes of particulars of employment, or gives an incom-

plete statement, then the employee can ask a tribunal to determine what particulars ought to have been included in the statement.

(ii) If there is a question regarding the accuracy of the terms in a section 1 statement or in a statement of changes of particulars of employment then either the employer or the employee can refer the matter to a tribunal. The tribunal can confirm or amend the particulars that have been given or substitute other particulars.

(iii) A claim can be brought at any time up to three months after the employment to which the question relates has finished or, if that is not reasonably practicable, within such further period as is reasonably practicable. (The 'not reasonably practicable' escape clause was inserted by TURERA.)

36.2   Itemised pay statement

Originally ss 8 to 10 EPCA (and s 11 re enforcement) as amended by TURERA. Now ss 8 to 10 ERA (and ss 11 and 12 re enforcement).

(a) *The right*

An employee is entitled to be given a written itemised pay statement. This must be given either before or at the time he is to be paid and must contain the following information:

(i) gross pay

(ii) the amounts of any deductions and the reasons why they have been made. (Where there are fixed deductions which are made from the employee's pay then a separate statement of these can be given to the employee in advance and the global amount of the fixed deductions is then noted on individual pay statements)

(iii) net pay, and

(iv) if different parts of the net amount are paid in different ways, the amount and method of payment of each bit.

(b) *Enforcement*

(i) If the employee is not given an itemised pay statement or if the statement is incomplete, the employee can refer the matter to a tribunal and the tribunal can decide what particulars ought to have been included in the statement.

(ii) Where a question arises as to the accuracy of an itemised pay statement or a statement of fixed deductions then either the employer or the employee can refer the matter to a tribunal. A tribunal cannot solely question the accuracy of an amount stated in the statement. In other words, the tribunal can look at the reasons for mistakes but not at the accuracy of the mathematics (although it can consider this under the Protection of wages provisions – see 36.3 below).

(iii) A claim can be brought at any time up to three months after the employee's employment finishes or, if that is not reasonably practicable, within such further period as is practical. (The 'not reasonably practicable' escape clause was inserted by TURERA.)

(iv) If the employee was not given a pay statement or if a pay statement or statement of fixed deductions did not contain the particulars required, the tribunal can make a declaration to that effect and can require the employer to pay the employee a sum not exceeding the amount of all the unnotified deductions that the employer made from the employee's pay during the 13 weeks immediately preceding the date when the application to the tribunal was made.

36.3 Protection of wages – unlawful deductions/payments to employers

Originally contained in the Wages Act 1986. Now ss 13 to 27 ERA. These provisions apply to payments employees make to employers as well as to deductions *per se.*

(a) *Meaning of 'wages'*

Wages are broadly any monetary sums paid by an employer payable by reference to the employee's employment other than items such as repayment of expenses. Both SSP and SMP are deemed to be 'wages' for these purposes.

(b) *Meaning of 'deduction'*

(i) Definition: A 'deduction' is, broadly, any shortfall between the amount that an employee is entitled to receive, after any lawful deductions have been made, and the amount he actually receives.

(ii) Exclusions from the definition of 'deduction':

- errors of computation
- deductions in respect of overpayment of wages or expenses
- deductions made following any statutory disciplinary procedure
- any requirement on the employer to deduct monies that have been determined to be due to a public authority
- agreed deductions from an employee's wages for the benefit of a third party
- deductions made by the employer in respect of strike or other industrial action taken by an employee
- any amount that the employee has agreed to repay to the employer by deduction from his wages pursuant to a court or tribunal order.

It should be noted that the above items are not necessarily lawful deductions – they are simply excluded from consideration under these particular statutory provisions.

(c) *When deductions are allowable*

For a deduction, which is caught by the Act, to be allowable it must satisfy one of the following criteria. It must either:

(i) be required or authorised by statute; or

(ii) be required or authorised by a provision of the worker's contract – which must have existed at the date when the matter giving rise to the deduction occurred; or

(iii) be a deduction to which the worker has previously signified his written agreement or consent. (Previous consent, in this context, means that consent must be given before the event which gives rise to the deduction being made rather than just pre-dating the deduction itself.)

(d) *Retail employment*

Where an employee is in 'retail employment', then no more than 10 per cent of his gross pay can be deducted from his wages on any pay day, in respect of cash shortages or stock losses. This limit is lifted in respect of wages paid for the employee's final period of employment – where there is no limit on the amount of any such deductions.

(e) *Bringing a claim*

A claim for wrongful deduction may be brought to an employment tribunal within three months of the deduction complained of.

36.4　Guarantee payments

Originally ss 12–18 EPCA, now ss 28–35 ERA.

(a) *The right*

(i)　Where an employer is unable to provide an employee with work through-out the whole of a day when the employee would normally be working be-cause of either:
  - a lack of work of the type which the employee is employed to do; or
  - any other occurrence affecting the work that the employee is employed to do; then

the employee is entitled to a guarantee payment in respect of that day.

(NB Where the employee's work spans midnight, the day on which the em-ployee must be 'workless' is the day in which the greater number of hours are normally worked. If the employee is employed for the same number of hours on both days then it is the second day that must be workless.)

(ii)　The amount of a guarantee payment is the employee's daily rate of pay subject to a statutory maximum, which is updated from time to time and is currently £14.50p per day. Any contractual pay which the employee is entitled to receive in respect of the same day goes towards discharging the employer's liability to pay a guarantee payment and vice versa.

(iii)　The maximum number of days for which guarantee payments can be made in any three-month period is the same as the number of days per week (not exceeding five) which the employee normally works.

(b) *Exclusions from the right to guarantee payments*

(i)　Employees who have not had at least one month's continuous service

(ii)　Employees employed:

(a)　under fixed-term contracts for less than three months; or

(b)　to do a specific task that is not expected to take more than three months unless they have been employed for three months

(ii)　If the failure to provide work is because of a strike or lock-out

(iv)　If the employee unreasonably refuses suitable alternative employment on the day in question; or if he fails to comply with his employer's reasonable re-quirements to ensure that his services are available on the day in question

(v) Where there is an exemption order, approved by the Secretary of State, in force in respect of the employee.

(c) *Enforcement*

A complaint regarding an employer's failure to pay all or part of an employee's guarantee payment entitlement can be presented to a tribunal within three months' of the employer's failure or, where that is not reasonably practicable, within such further time as is reasonably practicable.

36.5 Sunday working

When Sunday betting was legalised by the Deregulation and Contracting Out Act 1994, statutory protection similar to that in Schedule 4 of the Sunday Trading Act 1994, which covered shop workers, was enacted for betting workers by the Deregulation and Contracting Out Act 1994. This Act inserted a new Sch 5A into the Betting, Gaming and Lotteries Act 1963. The Sunday working provisions are now contained in ss 36 to 43, 45, 101, 104, 105(a), 108 and 197(2) ERA.

(a) *Who is covered?*

    (i)   These provisions apply only to those who work in England and Wales.

    (ii)   A 'betting worker' is a worker in England or Wales who can be required to do work either:

        (a) for a bookmaker at a track which includes dealing with betting transactions; or

        (b) in a licensed betting office on a day on which the office is open for betting transactions.

    (iii) A 'shop worker' is one who can be required to work in or about a shop on a day when the shop is open for serving customers.

(b) *'Protected shop/betting worker'*

    (i)   A 'protected shop/betting worker' is either:

        (a) one who was employed as a shop worker on 26 August 1994 or as a betting worker on 5 January 1995 (the commencement dates of the relevant provisions of the Sunday Trading Act 1994 and the Deregulation and Contracting Out Act 1994), but not to work only on Sundays, and has throughout his service from that date, until the date at which any particular right falls to be determined, continued to be a shop/betting worker; or

        (b) one who cannot be required under his contract of employment to work on Sundays (independently of any right to refuse to work on Sundays he may have under the Act).

    (ii)   While the employee remains a protected shop worker, however, the employer is entitled not to pay the employee for Sunday work. If there is no specific amount which is referable to the employee's Sunday work then the employer is entitled to reduce the employee's remuneration by the proportion of the week that the employee loses by no longer working on Sundays. If the work is made up during the remainder of the week then there will be no loss to the employee in such cases, but employers are entitled to reduce the protected employees' weekly hours by the number of hours that they normally worked on a Sunday.

(iii) A protected employee can be required to work on Sundays only if he has opted in to working on Sundays.

(c) *Opting in*

(i) A shop/betting worker is not a protected worker if
- he has given his employer an opting-in notice on or after the commencement date of the relevant statute; and
- after giving the notice, he has expressly agreed with his employer to do shop work, or betting work, on Sunday or on a particular Sunday.

(ii) An 'opting-in notice' is a written notice, signed and dated by the shop/betting worker, in which the worker expressly states that he wishes to work on Sunday or that he does not object to Sunday working.

(d) *Opting out*

(i) Any shop/betting worker who is not employed purely to work on Sundays, but who, under his contract, may be required to work on Sundays, is entitled to give his employer an opting-out notice. This is so even if the employee opted in to Sunday work.

(ii) An opting-out notice is a written notice, signed and dated by the employee, saying that the employee objects to Sunday working.

(iii) A shop/betting worker who is entitled to opt out of Sunday working must be given a notice in the following statutory form by his employer:

STATUTORY RIGHTS IN RELATION TO SUNDAY [SHOP/BETTING]
WORK

[You have become employed as a shop worker and are or can be required under your contract of employment to do the Sunday work your contract provides for.]
[You have become employed under a contract of employment under which you are or can be required to do Sunday betting work, that is to say, work—

at a track on a Sunday on which your employer is taking bets at the track, or

in a licensed betting office on a Sunday on which it is open for business.]

However, if you wish, you can give notice, as described in the next paragraph, to your employer and you will then have the right not to [work in or about a shop on any Sunday on which the shop is open] [do Sunday betting work on any Sunday] once three months have passed from the date on which you gave notice.

Your notice must—

be in writing;

be signed and dated by you;

say that you object to [Sunday working][doing Sunday betting work].

For three months after you give the notice, your employer can still require you to do all the Sunday work your contract provides for. After the three-month period has ended, you have the right to complain to an employment tribunal if, because of your refusal to [work on Sundays on which the shop is open] [do Sunday betting work], your employer—

> dismisses you, or

> does something else detrimental to you, for example, failing to promote you.

Once you have the rights described, you can surrender them only by giving your employer a further notice, signed and dated by you, saying that you wish to [work on Sunday] [do Sunday betting work] or that you do not object to [Sunday working] [doing Sunday betting work] and then agreeing with your employer to [work on Sundays] [do such work on Sundays] or on a particular Sunday.

(iv)   The above statement must be given to the employee within two months of the employee becoming an eligible shop/betting worker. If the employer fails to provide the statutory statement within two months then the three months' notice period during which the employee can normally be required to continue to work on Sundays is reduced to one month. This does not apply if the employee gives an opting-out notice before the two-month period for giving the statement expires.

(v)   An employee who opts out of Sunday working can still be required to work on Sundays during the three months' (or one month's – see iv above) statutory notice period before his opt-out takes effect.

(vi)   Where an employee has opted out of Sunday work then he can still opt back in again but, unless he does, any contractual requirement for Sunday work becomes unenforceable after the end of the notice period.

(e) *The rights*

    (i)   Dismissal for refusal to work on Sunday

       A protected or opted-out shop/betting worker is to be regarded as having been unfairly dismissed if the principal reason for dismissal is that he:

- refused, or proposed to refuse, to work on Sundays or a particular Sunday (provided that the Sunday in question is not during the notice period after the opting-out certificate has been given, but before it takes effect); or
- gave, or proposed to give, an opting-out notice to the employer.

       There is no minimum qualifying period of employment before the employee is entitled to bring such cases.

    (ii)   Selection for redundancy for refusal to work on Sunday

       A protected or opted-out shop/betting worker is to be regarded as having been unfairly dismissed if:

- the principal reason for dismissal is redundancy
- there are others holding similar positions who have not been dismissed; and
- the principal reason for his selection for dismissal was that he
  - refused, or proposed to refuse, to work on Sundays or a particular Sunday (provided that the Sunday in question is not during the notice period after the opting-out certificate has been given, but before it takes effect); or
  - gave, or proposed to give, an opting-out notice to the employer.

There is no minimum qualifying period of employment before the employee is entitled to bring such cases.

(iii) Right not to be subjected to a detriment for refusal to work on Sunday

A protected or opted-out shop/betting worker has the right not to be subjected to any detriment by his employer because the employee:

- refused, or proposed to refuse, to work on Sundays or on a particular Sunday (other than a Sunday during the notice period after an opting-out certificate has been given to an employer, but before it takes effect); or
- gave, or proposed to give, an opting-out notice to the employer.

These provisions do not apply where the detriment in question is the employee's dismissal, where the employee will have to claim unfair dismissal rather than a detriment. A detriment for these purposes includes any act, or deliberate failure to act, by the employer.

None of the following can amount to a detriment for these purposes:

- failure to pay the employee or to provide benefits in respect of Sunday work he has not done
- failure to provide the employee with work where the employer is statutorily allowed not to provide work (where a protected worker was obliged to work on Sunday but now does not, the employer is not obliged to provide alternative work or remuneration in lieu)
- the employer can offer to pay other protected or opted-out employees a premium for working on Sunday without either the failure to pay or the failure to offer the work being a detriment to anyone who is not made this offer
- the employer can offer to pay a protected or opted-out employee a premium for working on Sunday without either the failure to pay or the failure to offer being a detriment to anyone who refuses the offer.

Where an action continues over a period it is the beginning of that period which is relevant for deciding when that action occurred.

A deliberate failure to act is treated as having been done when it was either decided on or when the employer does an act inconsistent with the act he has failed to do.

(iv) Dismissal for asserting a statutory right

If an employee is dismissed for having brought a claim against the employer under these provisions then, provided:

- that the claim was brought in good faith, regardless of the merits of the claim, and
- that the employee made it clear in general terms what he was claiming,

the dismissal will be considered to be unfair.

36.6 Protection for health and safety representatives, trustees of pension schemes and employee representatives

(a) *Health and safety representatives*

Protection for health and safety representatives was originally introduced by

Sch 5 of TURERA to comply with the employment protection aspects of the Health and Safety European 'Framework Directive' (Directive 89/391/EEC). These rights were introduced by way of amendments to the EPCA mainly in: ss 22A to C, 57A and 59 – now ss 44, 48, 49, 100, 105, 108, 109 ERA and 117, 120, 125, 128, 130 and 132 ERA re remedies. These provisions were amended by the Health and Safety (Consultation with Employees) Regulations 1996 (SI 1996 No. 1513).

(I)   To whom and in what circumstances is protection afforded?

- Anyone designated by the employer to do anything connected with reducing or preventing health and safety risks, where the action taken by the employer is because they did anything to reduce or prevent a risk, or proposed to.
- Health and safety representatives and members of Safety Committees, who are either designated as such or who are acknowledged as such by the employer (under the Safety Representatives and Safety Committees Regulations 1977 SI 1977 No. 500 – SRSCR) and representatives of employee safety appointed under the Health and Safety (Consultation with Employees) Regulations 1996 SI 1996 No. 1513 – HSCER. Health and safety representatives and members of Safety Committees can be appointed, under SRSCR, where trade unions are recognised by the employer. Representatives of employee safety can be appointed under HSCER where no union is recognised.
- An employee who has action taken against him because he has brought something which he reasonably believes to be harmful or potentially harmful to health and safety to his employer's attention.

    An action in this type of case is available only where there are either no health and safety representatives or safety committees, or where it is not reasonably practicable for the employee to raise the matter through a safety representative or committee.
- An employee who has action taken against him because he left or proposed to leave, or refused to return to his place of work, or a dangerous part of it, because he reasonably believed there to be a serious and imminent danger which he could not have been expected to avert.
- An employee who has action taken against him because he took, or proposed to take, appropriate steps to protect himself or others in circumstances of danger which he reasonably believed to be serious and imminent.

In judging whether the steps the employee took were appropriate all the circumstances of the case must be looked at, including the employee's knowledge and the facilities and advice available to the employee. The employee loses his protection under this provision if the employer is able to show that the steps that the employee took were so negligent that the employer's treatment of him was reasonable in the circumstances.

LIVERPOOL JOHN MOORES UNIVERSITY
Aldham Robarts L.R.C.
TEL. 051 231 3701/3634

(ii) Rights
- Not to suffer a detriment by any deliberate act or inaction on the part of the employer.
- Dismissal for any of the above reasons is automatically unfair, as is selection for redundancy for those reasons where there are others holding similar positions who have not been dismissed. There is no qualifying period for entitlement to claim unfair dismissal, nor is there an upper age cut-off for entitlement to claim.

(iii) Remedies
A complaint must be brought within three months of the action complained of.

Detriment
- It is for the employer to show the reason for any action or failure to act.
- If the tribunal is satisfied that the employee has been treated detrimentally then the tribunal will make a declaration to that effect and award such compensation as is just and equitable.

Dismissal
- Where the employee has been designated by the employer to look after health and safety matters, is a health and safety representative or a member of a safety committee, then:
- As in the case of whistleblowers, there is no upper limit to the compensation that can be awarded in health and safety cases

(b) *Trustees of occupational pension schemes*
The rights and protection for trustees of occupational pension schemes were originally introduced by ss 42 to 46 of the Pensions Act 1995. These rights were introduced by way of amendments to the EPCA mainly in: ss 22A to C, 31A, 57, 57A, 59, 64, 71(2A and B), 72, 73, 75A and 77 to 79. These provisions are now ss 44, 48, 49, 58 to 60, 98(6), 100, 105, 108, 109, 117 to 122, 125, 128, 130 and 132 ERA.

(i) Right not to suffer a detriment or to be dismissed
- Employee trustees of occupational pension schemes related to their employment are entitled not to have any detrimental action taken against them by their employer (including any deliberate inaction), because they performed or proposed to perform any duties as trustees.
- The dismissal of employee trustees of occupational pension schemes or their selection for redundancy on those grounds (where there are others holding similar positions who have not been dismissed) will be automatically unfair and will attract special basic and compensatory awards (see under *Health and safety representatives* above). There is no qualifying period for entitlement to claim unfair dismissal on these grounds.

The general pattern of this protection is similar to the protection afforded in the case of health and safety representatives (see (a) above)

(ii)   Right to time off for occupational pension scheme trustees
- Employee occupational pension scheme trustees are entitled to be permitted reasonable paid time off:
    - to carry out their duties as trustees; or
    - for training relevant to their duties as trustees.
- The employee is entitled to be paid for time off under this provision as if he had been at work normally.
- The employee can complain to an employment tribunal if he is either refused time off or is not paid, or paid fully, for it.

(c) *Employee representatives*

The Collective Redundancies and Transfers of Undertaking (Protection of Employment) Regulations 1995 SI 1995/2587 introduced a new concept of elected 'Employee Representatives' whom the employer must consult on collective redundancies (see TULRA) and proposed transfers of undertakings (see Transfer of Undertakings (Protection of Employment) Regulations 1981) where no trade union is recognised. The regulations originally added protection for employee representatives into the EPCA by adding ss 22AA, 31AA and 57AA and making various amendments to other parts of the EPCA. These changes have now become ss 47, 61 to 63, 103, 105(6) ERA.

(i)   Right not to suffer a detriment or to be dismissed
- An employee representative, or someone who is a candidate to become an employee representative is entitled not to suffer a detriment because of anything that is done by him in carrying out his duties in respect of consultation with the employer either under TULRA or TOUR or as a candidate for election as an employee representative.
- The dismissal of employee representatives or their selection for redundancy on those grounds (where there are others holding similar positions who have not been dismissed) will be automatically unfair and will attract special basic and compensatory awards. There is no qualifying period for entitlement to claim unfair dismissal on these grounds.
- The general pattern of this protection is similar to the protection afforded in the case of health and safety representatives (see (a) above).

(ii)   Right to time off

Employee representatives and candidates for election as employee representatives are entitled to be permitted reasonable paid time off:
- to carry out their duties as employee representatives; or
- in connection with their candidacy.

The employee can complain to an employment tribunal if he is either refused time off or is not paid, or paid fully, for it.

36.7   Time off for public duties

Originally s 29 EPCA (and s 30 re enforcement). Now ss 50 ERA (and s 51 re-enforcement).

(i)   JPs are entitled to time off to perform any of the duties of their office.

(ii) Members of
- local authorities
- statutory tribunals
- police authorities including the Service Authority for National Criminal Intelligence Service and the Service Authority for the Crime Squad (this extended meaning of 'police authority' was brought in by the Police Act 1997)
- boards of prison visitors or prison visiting committees
- certain health bodies
- certain education bodies
- the Environment Agency or the Scottish Environment Protection Agency

are allowed to have time off to attend meetings of the body (including committees and sub-committees) and to do anything else for the purpose of discharging the functions of the body in question or its committees.

(iii) The amount of time that an employee is allowed is what is reasonable, and depends *inter alia* on:
- the amount of time off that an employee has for trade union activities and duties;
- the amount of time off required for the public duties in question; and
- the needs of the employer's business.

(iv) Time off under this provision is unpaid.

36.8 Suspension on medical grounds

Originally ss 19 to 22 EPCA. Now ss 64, 65 and 69 ERA (and s 70 re enforcement).

(a) *Who is entitled*

An employee who is suspended because of a requirement imposed by
- (i) Regulation 16 of the Control of Lead at Work Regulations 1980
- (ii) Regulation 16 of the Ionising Radiation Regulations 1985; or
- (iii) Regulation 11 of the Control of Substances Hazardous to Health Regulations 1988.

(b) *The rights*

(i) The employee is entitled to be paid his normal remuneration for up to 26 weeks.

(ii) An employee who is dismissed because of a requirement to suspend him on medical grounds can claim unfair dismissal if he had one month's continuous service before the date of dismissal.

(iii) Where an employer dismisses a replacement who has been hired to cover for such an employee, then provided
- that the employer informed the replacement in writing that he was being hired to cover for someone on medical suspension and would be dismissed when that person returned; and
- that the employer dismisses the replacement to take the suspended employee back

the employer will be deemed to have a 'substantial' reason for dismissal. The employer will still have to satisfy the tribunal that they acted reasonably in dismissing the replacement in the circumstances.

(c) *Exclusions from the right to remuneration*

The following are excluded from entitlement to remuneration while under medical suspension:

(i)   those who have been continuously employed for less than one month before being suspended

(ii)   those on a fixed-term contract of three months or less, provided they have not been employed for more than three months

(iii)   those hired for a job that is expected to take three months or less, provided they have not been employed for more than three months

(iv)   an employee who is sick

(v)   an employee who unreasonably refuses to undertake suitable alternative employment

(vi)   an employee who unreasonably refuses to comply with the employer's reasonable requirements for keeping his services available.

36.9   Rights connected with pregnancy and maternity

(a) *Time off for ante-natal care*

Introduced by the Employment Act 1980, originally adding a new s 31A to the EPCA. These provisions are now contained in ss 55 to 57 ERA.

(i)   An employee who is pregnant and who has made an appointment to attend for ante-natal care on the advice of a medical practitioner, midwife or health visitor is entitled to take paid time off during working hours to keep the appointment

(ii)   Except for the first antenatal appointment, the employee must show the employer, if he asks for it:

- a certificate from a medical practitioner, midwife or health visitor to say that she is pregnant; and
- an appointment card or document showing that an ante-natal appointment has been made.

(iii)   An employee can complain to an employment tribunal

- that she has unreasonably been refused time off; or
- that her employer has refused to pay her fully or at all for the time she has taken off for ante-natal care.

(iv)   If a tribunal finds that a woman has been unreasonably refused time off, then, as well as declaring that to be the case, it must also award the woman the remuneration that the employer would have paid her if she had not been refused the time off.

(b) *Suspension on maternity grounds*

The right to payment on suspension on maternity grounds was added to the EPCA by TURERA as ss 45 to 47 EPCA. The provisions are now contained in ss 66 to 70 ERA.

(i) An employee is suspended on maternity grounds if she is suspended pursuant to an Order specified under s 66(2) ERA on the ground that she is pregnant, has recently given birth or is breast-feeding a child. Currently there is one Order made under this provision: Suspension From Work (On Maternity Grounds) Order 1994 (SI 1994/2930) which in turn refers to a list of reasons for suspension under this heading. The reasons for suspension are contained in Regs 13A and 13B Management of Health and Safety at Work Regulations 1992 (SI 1992/2051) (introduced by the Management of Health and Safety at Work (Amendment) Regulations 1994 (SI 1994/2865) and in Annexes 1 and 2 of EC Directive 92/85/EEC – the Pregnant Workers Directive.

(ii) As an alternative to suspension, the employee has a right to be offered any alternative employment that the employer has available. For alternative employment to be 'suitable' for these purposes it must be
- suitable in relation to the employee
- appropriate for her to do in the circumstances; and
- on terms and conditions not substantially less favourable than her existing terms and conditions.

(iii) An employee is entitled to be paid while she is suspended on maternity grounds. Any contractual payment made by the employer goes towards discharging the employer's liability to pay the woman while on suspension so that if the employee does any work for the employer, the remuneration due to her on suspension will 'top up' her pay to the extent that it is less than her normal 'week's pay'.

(iv) It should be noted that if an employee is dismissed in circumstances where she ought to be suspended under these provisions, she will be able to claim that her dismissal is automatically unfair. It will also be automatically unfair to select a woman for redundancy because of her entitlement to be suspended because of pregnancy where there are others holding similar positions who have not been dismissed.

(c) *Right to maternity leave for all employees*
A general right to maternity leave, for all women regardless of service, was introduced by TURERA. The purpose of this was to give effect to the Pregnant Workers' Directive 92/85/EEC. TURERA gave effect to these changes by inserting new ss 33 to 38A into the EPCA. The provisions are now contained in ss 71 to 78 ERA.

(i) The right
There is a general right for employees to have 14 weeks' maternity leave regardless of the length of time for which they have been employed by their employer provided that they comply with all the notification requirements. Where an employee has a contractual right to maternity leave then she can pick-and-mix her contractual and statutory rights to give herself the best composite right.

(ii) Notification requirements

- At least 21 days before her Maternity Leave Period (MLP) commences the employee must inform her employer:
  - that she is pregnant
  - of the expected week of childbirth (EWC) (or, if childbirth has already occurred, the date on which it occurred)
  - of a date, no earlier than the beginning of the 11th week before the EWC when the employee intends her absence to begin. But
    - where the employee's first day of absence for her MLP is the first day after the beginning of the sixth week before EWC, the employee need not give advance notice of her intended absence, but must inform the employer as soon as is reasonably practicable that she is away from work due to pregnancy
    - where the employee's MLP begins on the day of childbirth she need inform her employer only that she has given birth as soon as is reasonably practicable after the birth.
- Notification of absence or intended absence must be in writing if the employer so requests.
- If the employee is entitled, and wishes, to exercise her right to return later than the end of the MLP, within 29 weeks of the week of childbirth, then she must also inform her employer that she intends to exercise that right. (For the right to return after the MLP for those with more than two years' service at the 11th week before EWC see (d) below.)
- If the employer asks her to, the employee must provide a certificate from a doctor or midwife stating the EWC.

(iii) Commencement of maternity leave period

The MLP commences with whichever is the first of the following events:
- the date at which the employee has notified her employer that her MLP will begin
- the first day after the beginning of the sixth week before the EWC on which she is absent from work wholly or partly because of pregnancy
- in any other case the date of childbirth.

(iv) Continuation of contract

An employee who has fulfilled the notification requirements and who is absent from work during her MLP is entitled to the terms and conditions of her employment, other than remuneration, as if she was not absent and had not been pregnant or given birth to a child.

(v) Duration of the MLP

The MLP lasts for 14 weeks from its commencement or until at least two weeks after the birth of the child if later (the ban on an employee working within two weeks starting with the date of childbirth was introduced by Maternity (Compulsory Leave) Regulations 1994 (SI 1994/2479)).

(vi) Return after maternity leave

An employee who wants to return to work before the end of her MLP must give her employer at least seven days' notice of her proposed return date. If the employee tries to return without giving seven days' notice the employer can postpone her return so that he effectively has seven days' notice of her return. This is subject to a proviso that the employer cannot postpone the employee's return beyond the end of her 14 weeks' MLP.

(vii) Redundancy during the maternity leave period

If there is a redundancy during the maternity leave period then the employee is entitled to be offered any suitable alternative employment which is available on terms and conditions that are not substantially less beneficial than those she enjoyed under her previous contract.

If the employer fails to offer suitable alternative employment that is available or if the employee is selected for redundancy because of any reason connected with her pregnancy or maternity leave (where there are others holding similar positions who have not been dismissed), the employee will be automatically treated as having been unfairly dismissed. If an employee has a right to return within 29 weeks of the birth and is either unfairly dismissed or made redundant, during or at the end of her MLP, then it is a condition of entitlement to exercise her right to return that she repays the employer any unfair dismissal compensation or redundancy payment paid, if he asks her to.

(d) *Right to return to work after extended maternity leave*

The right to maternity leave in the EPCA, for employees with more than two years' service, was significantly amended by TURERA and new ss 39 to 44 were substituted in EPCA. These provisions are now contained in ss 79 to 85 ERA.

(i) The right

The 'right to return' is the right of an employee to return to work at any time from the end of her Maternity Leave Period (MLP) up to 29 weeks after the beginning of the week in which childbirth occurs.

To be entitled to this 'right to return' the employee must:

- fulfil the requirements to be entitled to maternity leave (see (c) above)
- have notified her employer that she intends to exercise her right to return to work; and
- at the beginning of the 11th week before the expected week of childbirth (EWC) have been continuously employed for at least two years.

Where the employee has a contractual right to return then she can pick-and-mix her contractual and statutory rights to give herself the best composite right.

(ii) Notification requirements

As well as fulfilling the notification requirements before the start of her MLP (see (c)(ii) above), the employer can ask for written confirmation that the employee still wishes to exercise her right to return.

Such a request:
- cannot be made earlier than 21 days before the end of the MLP
- must be in writing
- must state that if the employee does not answer the request within 14 days, or if that is not reasonably practicable, within such further time as is reasonably practicable, she will lose her right to return.

The employee must give 21 days' written notice of her intended return date.

(iii) Postponing the return

The employer may postpone the employee's return for up to four weeks after the notified day of return (NDR) if he notifies the employee:
- of the specific reason for delaying her return; and
- of the date, not more than four weeks after the NDR, when the employee can return to work.

An employee unable to return owing to sickness can postpone her return for up to four weeks after her NDR (or after the 29-week period if no NDR has been notified):
- she must provide her employer with a medical certificate before the NDR (or the end of the 29-week period if no NDR)
- the certificate must specify that she is unable to return due to illness
- this right to delay can be exercised only once.

Where there is an interruption of work, due to industrial action or otherwise, such that it is not reasonable to expect the employee to return at her NDR or at the end of the 29-week period:
- if the employee has notified her intended return date, she may return when work resumes or as soon as is reasonably practicable afterwards
- if the employee has not notified her intended return date, she may exercise her right to return so that she returns within 28 days of the end of the interruption of work.

(iv) Return to what?

The employee's primary right to return is a right to return to work
- with the employer by whom she was employed at the end of her MLP; or
- with his successor
- in the job in which she was employed before she went on maternity leave
- on terms and conditions as to remuneration no less favourable than if she had not been absent
- with seniority, pension and similar rights as if her employment up to the end of her MLP was continuous with her employment after her return (subject to credits in certain cases under Social Security Act 1989 schedule 5)
- otherwise on terms and conditions as if she had not been absent after her maternity leave period.

(v) Redundancy before return date

If it is not reasonably practicable by reason of redundancy to permit the employee to return to work, she is entitled to be offered any suitable alternative employment that is available on terms and conditions that are not substantially less beneficial than those she enjoyed under her previous contract.

If the employer:

- fails to offer suitable alternative employment that is available; or
- selects an employee for redundancy for any reason connected with pregnancy or childbirth, where there are others holding similar positions who have not been dismissed

the employee will be treated as having been automatically unfairly dismissed.

If an employee has a right to return within 29 weeks of the birth and is either unfairly dismissed or made redundant, during or at the end of her MLP, then it is a condition of her entitlement to exercise her right to return that she repays the employer any unfair dismissal compensation or redundancy payment paid, if he asks her to.

(vi) Failure to permit a woman to return after maternity leave and dismissal

These provisions were originally contained in s 56 EPCA. The Employment Act 1980 made major amendments adding s 56A to the EPCA. TURERA made further minor amendments. These provisions are now contained in s 96 ERA.

- Where a woman is not allowed to return to work after extended maternity leave (assuming she has satisfied all the notification requirements), then she is, *prima facie*, treated as having been dismissed for the reason for which she was not allowed to return to work; and she is treated as having been employed up to her NRD.
- There are two exceptions to this general position:
  - Where the employer employs five or fewer employees immediately before the end of her MLP (including any employees employed by any associated employers).

    If in such cases it is not reasonably practicable for the employer (or his successor):

    - to offer suitable alternative employment; or
    - to allow the woman to return to her original job

    then the woman will not be treated as having been dismissed.

- If it is not reasonably practicable, for a reason other than redundancy, for the woman to be allowed to return to her original job and
  - the employer or a successor of his offers the woman suitable alternative employment and
  - she accepts or unreasonably refuses that offer

  then, again, the woman will not be treated as having been dismissed by ˙ʳ refused the right to return to work.

(e) *Dismissal of a temporary replacement*

This was originally contained in s 61 EPCA, was subject to minor amendment by TURERA, and is now contained in s 106 ERA.

Where a temporary replacement is engaged to do the work of an employee who is:

- suspended on maternity grounds; or
- absent because of pregnancy or confinement

then, provided:

- the replacement is informed of this fact when they take the job on; and
- the replacement is dismissed to allow for the woman to return to work

the employer will be seen to have a substantial reason for dismissing the employee in relation to unfair dismissal legislation. The employer will still have to show, of course, that they acted fairly in treating that reason as a sufficient reason for dismissal.

(f) *Right not to be dismissed because of pregnancy or childbirth*

A limited right in the EPCA, making dismissal for pregnancy automatically unfair in certain circumstances, was amended by TURERA which inserted a new s 60 into the EPCA. This right is now contained in s 99 ERA.

An employee is considered to be automatically unfairly dismissed if she is dismissed:

- for any reason related to her pregnancy
- where her MLP is ended for any reason connected with
  - the fact that she has given birth to a child; or
  - the fact that she took maternity leave or the benefits attached to it
- when she ought to have been suspended on maternity grounds
- where her MLP (or extended maternity period) is ended by dismissal because of redundancy and she was not offered suitable alternative employment which was available; or
- where she is ill at the end of her maternity leave, has given the employer a medical certificate covering the period of her illness (up to four weeks) and she is dismissed during the currency of the medical certificate.

(g) *Right to pay in lieu of notice while absent due to the pregnancy or maternity*

Employees who are given notice when they are away from work due to pregnancy or confinement are entitled to be paid in lieu of notice provided that their notice entitlement is not over a week more than the statutory minimum notice entitlement.

Any sick pay, SSP, maternity pay, SMP or holiday pay goes towards discharging the employer's obligations as do State sickness benefits.

Where it was the employee who gave notice, the requirement for the employer to pay for the notice period in such cases only applies if the employee actually leaves the employer's employment.

(h) *Automatic right to written reasons for dismissal in pregnancy and maternity cases*

This provision became s 53(2A) EPCA by an amendment made by TURERA and is now s 92(4) ERA.

A woman who is dismissed while pregnant or in trying to exercise her right to return to work is entitled to be given written reasons for dismissal without asking for them.

36.10 Notice rights

Originally contained in ss 49 to 52 and Schedule 3 EPCA, Social Security and Housing Benefits Act 1982, Social Security (Incapacity for Work) Act 1994 and TURERA. These are now contained in ss 86 to 91 ERA.

(a) *General right*

(i)	Employees who have been employed for more than four weeks and less than two years are entitled to a minimum of one week's notice to terminate their contracts of employment. After completing two years' continuous employment an employee is entitled to a minimum of two weeks' notice with an extra week per completed year of service up to 12 weeks' after 12 completed years of service.

(ii)	Employees who have been employed for more than four weeks must give a minimum of one week's notice to terminate their contracts of employment.

(b) *Right to pay in lieu of notice*

(i)	An employee who gives or who is given notice and who

- is ready and willing to work, but is not given any work by his employer
- is incapable of work because of sickness or injury
- is absent from work wholly or partly because of pregnancy or child-birth, or
- is absent from work on holiday

is entitled to be paid in lieu of notice provided that his notice entitlement is not over a week more than the statutory minimum notice entitlement.

(ii)	Any sick pay, SSP, maternity pay, SMP or holiday pay goes towards dis-charging the employer's obligations as do State sickness benefits. If the employee gives notice of termination then the requirement for the employer to pay for the notice period in such cases applies only if the employee actually leaves the employer's employment.

(iii)	The right to be paid in lieu of notice ceases if, and when, an employee is guilty of gross misconduct and could therefore be summarily dismissed, or if the employee takes part in a strike.

36.11 Written reasons for dismissal

Previously s 53 EPCA as extended by TURERA in respect of pregnant women and those dismissed on maternity leave – now s 92 ERA.

(a) *General right*

(i)	An employee who has been employed for not less than one year before being dismissed is entitled to request written reasons for dismissal. (The erstwhile requirement for two years' continuous employment was re-duced to one year with effect from 1 June 1999 by Unfair Dismissal and

Statement of Reasons for Dismissal (Variation of Qualifying Period) Order 1999 SI 1999 No. 1436.)
(ii) Where such a request is made the employer must provide written reasons within 14 days of the request.
(b) *Pregnancy and childbirth*
An employee who is pregnant when dismissed or whose maternity leave period ends by reason of dismissal is entitled to be provided with written reasons for dismissal automatically.

36.12 Unfair dismissal

Provisions concerning unfair dismissal are derived from: Betting Gaming and Lotteries Act 1963, EPCA, Employment Acts 1980, 1982 and 1989, Sex Discrimination Act 1986, TURERA, Sunday Trading Act 1994, Deregulation and Contracting Out Act 1994, TULRA, Collective Redundancies and Transfer of Undertakings (Protection of Employment) (Amendment) Regulations 1995 (SI 1995/2587), Pensions Act 1995. These rights are now contained in:

- ss 94 to 110 dealing with qualification to claim and the circumstances in which an unfair dismissal claim can be brought
- ss 111 to 134 dealing with bringing an unfair dismissal claim and remedies for unfair dismissal.

(a) *General right*
(i) Entitlement to claim
There is a general right for employees not to be unfairly dismissed. To be entitled to claim unfair dismissal the employee:
- must have more than one year's continuous service (The erstwhile requirement for two years' continuous employment was reduced to one year with effect from 1 June 1999 by Unfair Dismissal and Statement of Reasons for Dismissal (Variation of Qualifying Period) Order 1999 SI 1999 No. 1436)
- must be under 'normal retirement age' for an employee in that organisation or if there is no normal retirement age, under 65
- must be normally employed to work in Great Britain
- must not be employed under a fixed-term contract with a valid exclusion against claiming unfair dismissal entered into before 25 October 1999 other than where the claim is for unfair dismissal related to pregnancy, childbirth or assertion of a statutory right when even an earlier exclusion is invalid (These changes in the right to exclude unfair dismissal claims were brought into effect by the Employment Relations Act 1999)
- must not be dismissed while taking part in industrial action
- must be 'dismissed'. A dismissal occurs where:
  - an employee is dismissed with or without notice
  - a fixed-term contract expires without being renewed on the same terms

- an employee is 'constructively dismissed' – ie he is entitled to leave because the employer fundamentally breaches his contract of employment
- an employee who is under notice gives counter-notice to the employer which expires earlier than the employer's original notice.

(ii)   The elements of unfair dismissal

Where there is an unfair dismissal claim it is for the employer to show the tribunal:

- the principal reason for dismissing the employee
- that the reason for dismissal was one of the following
  - related to the employee's capability or qualifications to do the work for which he was employed
  - related to the employee's conduct
  - the employee was redundant, or
  - there was a statutory bar on the employee continuing to work in the position that he held or the reason was some other substantial reason that would justify the dismissal of an employee holding the position that that employee held.

It is then for the tribunal to decide (rather than the onus being on either party to satisfy it) that the employer acted fairly in dismissing the employee for that reason.

In determining:

- what the principal reason for dismissal was
- whether it was a sufficient reason to justify the dismissal of the employee; or
- whether the dismissal was fair or not

no account is to be taken of any pressure exerted on the employer by way of industrial action or threatened industrial action.

(b) *Special cases*

(i)   Failure to allow a woman to return after maternity leave

This is dealt with under maternity rights. It applies to cases where a woman who has a right to return to work after extended maternity leave (ie the right to return within 29 weeks of the birth of her child) is not allowed to return to work. In such cases she is treated as having been dismissed on her notified day of return.

Where the employee is dismissed in a redundancy situation without being offered alternative work which is available then her dismissal is automatically unfair.

In other cases the fairness of the dismissal must be judged by considering whether the employer would have been acting reasonably or unreasonably in treating [the reason for dismissal] as a sufficient reason for dismissing the employee if she had not been absent from work. It should be noted that the dismissal of a temporary replacement for a woman who

has been on maternity leave or who is suspended on maternity grounds
is deemed to be for a substantial reason provided:
- that the person was told in writing that they were going to be a temporary replacement; and
- the person is dismissed so that the woman can resume work.

(The employer will still have to show that the dismissal of the temporary replacement was fair in all the circumstances of the case.)

(ii) Dismissal related to pregnancy or childbirth

An employee is considered to be automatically unfairly dismissed if she is dismissed for reasons related to pregnancy or childbirth or having taken maternity leave. (See mainly under rights connected with pregnancy and maternity above.)

(iii) Dismissal in health and safety cases

Employees who are dismissed because:
- they are health and safety representatives
- they are representatives of employee safety
- they are members of a health and safety committee
- they have brought a health and safety issue to the employer's notice
- they have taken steps to protect themselves or others; or
- they have left work where they perceive a serious danger to health and safety

are treated as having been automatically unfairly dismissed. (See also *Rights of health and safety representatives* – 36.6(a) above.)

(iv) Shop workers/betting workers

Shop or betting workers who are dismissed for refusing to work on a Sunday or Sundays or for giving or proposing to give their employer an opting-out certificate are considered to be automatically unfairly dismissed (see mainly under *Sunday working* – 36.5 above).

(v) Pension scheme trustees

Employees who are trustees of the occupational pension scheme who are dismissed for being trustees or for undertaking any of the duties as such are considered to be automatically unfairly dismissed (see mainly under *Trustees of occupational pension schemes* – 36.6(b) above).

(vi) Employee representatives

Employees who are dismissed for being employee representatives (ie those elected for purposes of being consulted in relation to proposed redundancies or the transfer of an undertaking) or for standing for election as employee representatives are considered to be automatically unfairly dismissed (see mainly under *Employee representatives* – 36.6(c) above)

(vii) Assertion of a statutory right

An employee who is dismissed because:
- he brought proceedings to enforce a relevant statutory right of his against the employer; or

- he alleged that the employer had infringed a relevant statutory right of his is considered to be automatically unfairly dismissed. It does not matter for these purposes
- whether the employee actually has that statutory right or if it has been infringed provided that the claim is made in good faith
- if a specific claim is not made – provided it is reasonably clear to the employer what right it is being claimed was infringed.

The relevant statutory rights are:

- any right under the ERA whose remedy is by way of complaint to an employment tribunal
- a claim for minimum notice
- the right not to have unauthorised deductions of TU subscriptions or contributions to the union's political fund made
- action short of dismissal for trade union membership
- time off for trade union duties or activities or payment for time off for trade union duties

(viii) Selection for redundancy for certain reasons

- Where an employee is selected for redundancy in circumstances where the redundancy applies to other employees who have not been dismissed; and
- the reason for selection is one of a number of unacceptable reasons

then the employee's dismissal is automatically unfair.

The unacceptable reasons for these purposes are, broadly, those set out in paragraphs i to vii above:

- the employee was selected for redundancy because of a reason related to maternity or pregnancy
- the employee was selected for redundancy for health and safety reasons
- the employee was a shop or betting worker and was selected for redundancy for a reason related to not wishing to work on Sundays
- the employee was a trustee of an occupational pension scheme and was selected for redundancy for a reason related to carrying out his duties in respect of the scheme
- the employee was an employee representative or seeking election as such and was selected for redundancy for a reason related to carrying out his duties as an employee representative or in connection with seeking election
- the employee was selected for redundancy because he had asserted a relevant statutory right against his employer.

(c) *Complaint to a tribunal*

An employee may present an unfair dismissal complaint to an employment tribunal within three months of the date of dismissal or, if that is not reasonably practicable, within such further time as the tribunal considers to be reasonably practicable.

(d) *Remedies*
  (i) Reinstatement and re-engagement
       If a tribunal finds that an unfair dismissal complaint is made out then it must explain to the employee the orders that it can make for reinstatement and re-engagement and ask the employee if he wishes the tribunal to make such an order.
       - Reinstatement – an order for reinstatement is that the employee be put back into the position in which he would have been if he had not been dismissed.
       - Re-engagement – an order for re-engagement is that the employee be put into a different job from that from which he was dismissed. In the case of re-engagement the tribunal will set out the terms on which the employee is to be re-engaged.

       If the employer unreasonably fails to comply with an order for reinstatement or re-engagement then the tribunal will award compensation. The amount that is awarded can be increased by an additional award, which will be:
       - in a case where the dismissal amounted to unlawful sex or race discrimination – an extra 26 to 52 weeks' pay; and
       - in any other case – an extra 13 to 26 weeks' pay.

       An additional award cannot be made where the employee is entitled to a 'Special' basic and compensatory award.
  (ii) Compensation
       Compensation is broadly of two types – the basic award and the compensatory award. In addition, in some cases where the employer unreasonably fails to comply with a reinstatement or re-engagement order then the tribunal can award an additional award.

       The basic award

       The basic award is equivalent to a redundancy payment, ie:
       - 1½ weeks' pay for each year of service over the age of 41
       - 1 week's pay for each year of service over the age of 22
       - ½ week's pay per year of service at any lower age.

       The statutory limit for a week's pay applies.

       Only the best 20 years of service can be counted under this provision.

       From the age of 64 the complainant loses 1/12 of this entitlement per month over 64 – this is to allow for the fact that at age 65 there would be no entitlement.

       The compensatory award

       The compensatory award is to compensate the complainant for the loss that he has suffered by being unfairly dismissed insofar as that loss is attributable to action taken by the employer.

       The compensatory award is subject to an upper limit. The Employment Relations Act provided for the upper limit to be set at £50,000 and for it to be index-linked from 1999.

The losses that can be compensated include:

- any expenses incurred by the employee as a result of his dismissal; and
- the loss of any benefit that the employee might have expected to have had if it were not for the dismissal, including any redundancy payment in excess of the statutory amount that the employee might otherwise have expected to have.

Some factors may reduce the compensation that the employee is ultimately awarded:

- The complainant is under a duty to mitigate the losses arising from the dismissal.
- The tribunal can reduce the compensatory award, to such degree as it considers just and equitable, where the employee has in any way contributed to his own dismissal.

If the employer has given the employee any payment on the grounds that the dismissal was on account of redundancy then the amount by which that payment exceeds the basic award is to be taken to reduce the compensatory award.

36.13   Redundancy payments

Previously Part VI EPCA amended by Employment Acts 1982 and 1989 and TUR-ERA. Now ss 136 to 181 ERA.

(a) *General right*

    (i)   Dismissal for redundancy

        An employee is dismissed for redundancy if he is dismissed wholly or mainly because:

- the employer stops running the business for which the employee was employed
- the employer moves it to a different place; or
- the requirement for employees to carry out the type of work that the employee can be asked to do ceases or diminishes.

    (ii)   Lay off and short-time working as redundancy

        There are complex provisions under which an employee who has been laid off or kept on 'short time' (ie earning less than half his normal weekly wage because of lay off) can give notice to his employer claiming a redundancy payment if that situation continues for four weeks or for six weeks in a 13-week period. The employer can give a counter-notice disputing liability to pay a redundancy payment. The most usual case where this will be relevant is where the employer informs the employee that there is a likelihood of not less than 13 weeks' full employment, which will begin within four weeks of the date of the employer's counter-notice. Where such full-time employment is available the employee will not be entitled to a redundancy payment.

(b) *Qualifications for entitlement*

- The employee must be continuously employed for two years.
- The employee must be either:

- below normal retiring age for employees of that type in the bu.. question; or
- below 65.

Where the employee is over 64 he loses 1/12 of his redundancy payment for every month over 64.

(c) *Amount of redundancy payment*

A redundancy payment is 1½ weeks' pay for each year of employment over the age of 41. One week's pay for every year over the age of 22 and ½ week's pay for any year below 22. The maximum number of years that can be taken into account in calculating a redundancy payment is 20 and the amount of 'a week's pay' is limited by statute.

(d) *Exclusions from entitlement*

   (i)   Summary dismissal

An employee is not entitled to a redundancy payment if he is or could be summarily dismissed unless:

- the reason for dismissal is that he has taken part in a strike; or
- he is dismissed during the minimum notice which he is entitled to be given by the employer by statute in which case it is for the tribunal to decide what redundancy payment, if any, the employee ought to get.

   (ii) New employment and the trial period

If the employee accepts or unreasonably refuses suitable alternative employment then he is not entitled to a redundancy payment.

Where, before the employee's employment terminates, he is offered new employment to begin within four weeks of the end of his current employment, then

- if the terms and conditions of the new contract are different from the old contract the employee has a four-week statutory trial period in which to decide whether or not to continue in the job. If he does not, or if the employer dismisses him for a reason arising out of the new terms and conditions, then he is considered to have been dismissed from the original redundancy date
- where the employee needs retraining, a longer trial period can be agreed in writing between the employer and the employee.

(e) *Claiming a redundancy payment*

A claim for a redundancy payment must be made within six months of dismissal to a tribunal or to the employer. If a claim is made late, within a year of the dismissal, then the tribunal can award a redundancy payment if it appears to the tribunal to be just and equitable that the payment should be made. It should be noted that if the employer becomes insolvent or fails to pay the employee a redundancy payment to which he is entitled, a claim may be made directly to the Secretary of State for a redundancy payment to be paid.

36.14   Insolvency

Originally in EPCA as amended by Insolvency Act 1985 and 1986, Bankruptcy (Scotland) Act 1985, Employment Acts 1989 and 1990 and TURERA, now ss 182 to 190 ERA.

These provisions allow for the payment of certain debts owed to an employee by an employer who becomes insolvent to be paid by the Secretary of State.

36.15   Agreements to exclude the protection of the ERA

(a) *Fixed-term contracts*

Where the employee is under a fixed-term contract of one year or more, entitlement to claim unfair dismissal can be excluded.

Where the employee is under a fixed-term contract of two years or more, entitlement to claim a redundancy payment can be excluded.

(b) *Compromise agreements*

Introduced by TURERA.

Generally, the rights under employment legislation, including those under the ERA, cannot be contracted out of. TURERA introduced a new system whereby a valid agreement can be reached to exclude an employee's rights to claim provided that a solicitor or barrister is involved and that certain specific statutory requirements are adhered to. (A settlement of a case can still be validly reached with the assistance of a Conciliation Officer.)

36A   Employment Rights (Dispute Resolution) Act 1998

Amends Courts Act 1971, Sex Discrimination Act 1975, Race Relations Act 1976, Trade Union and Labour Relations (Consolidation) Act 1992, Disability Discrimination Act 1995, Employment Tribunals Act 1996, Employment Rights Act 1996, Trade Union Reform and Employment Rights Act 1993

- Changes the name of industrial tribunals to employment tribunals
- Makes provisions allowing unfair dismissal cases to be dealt with by binding arbitration if both parties agree to this way of dealing with them
- Allows for trade union officials and those working in advice centres to advise on compromise agreements, as well as qualified lawyers, provided:
  - that they are certified by the union or advice centre as competent to give advice and as competent to do so on behalf of the union or advice centre; and
  - that the claim being compromised is not against the union or advice centre in question
- Provides for reduction of the unfair dismissal compensatory award where the employer provides an appeals procedure which the employee has not used. The tribunal can reduce the employee's compensation in such cases by such amount as it considers just and equitable having regard to all the circumstances of the case including the likelihood of the employee being successful on appeal subject to a maximum deduction of two weeks' pay. If the employer prevents the employee from appealing against dismissal then the tribunal may enhance his compensatory award by up to two weeks' pay.

An amendment is made so that an employee can obtain a higher additional award, equivalent to that available in race and sex discrimination cases, where an unfair dismissal is also disability discrimination.

37   Employment Subsidies Act 1978

Allows for payments to be made to employers under schemes to alleviate unemployment. There have been two schemes set up under this Act in Great Britain, the Temporary Employment Subsidy and the Youth Employment Subsidy.

37A   Employment Tribunals Act 1996

Name changed by Employment Rights (Dispute Resolution) Act 1998 from Industrial Tribunals Act 1996 Repeals and consolidates various provisions from EPCA, TULRA and TURERA. Amended by the Employment Rights (Dispute Resolution) Act 1998, National Minimum Wage Act 1998.

Consolidates the legislation dealing with the powers and constitution of employment tribunals and the Employment Appeals Tribunal (EAT) and with conciliation and compromise agreements in tribunal cases.

37B   Employment Tribunals Extension of Jurisdiction (England and Wales) Order 1994 (SI 1994/1623)/(Scotland – SI 1994/1624)

Name changed by Employment Rights (Dispute Resolution) Act 1998 from Industrial Tribunals Extension of Jurisdiction (England and Wales) Order 1994. Extends the jurisdiction of employment tribunals as originally provided for by s 131 EPCA which, as amended by TURERA, is now s 3 Employment Tribunals Act 1996.

Allows for breach of contract claims to be brought to an employment tribunal where the claim arises or is in issue on termination of employment.

The limit on such claims is £25,000. Certain types of claim, such as those involving personal injuries and restraint of trade, are excluded from the tribunal's jurisdiction. A claim under these provisions must be brought within three months of the date of dismissal or within such further time as is reasonably practicable where it is not reasonably practicable to meet the three-month time limit. The respondent can also make a counter-claim against the applicant within six weeks of receiving the notice of the applicant's originating application.

37C   Employment Tribunals Rules of Procedure (Amendment) Rules 1996

Name changed by Employment Rights (Dispute Resolution) Act 1998 from Industrial Tribunals Rules of Procedure (Amendment) Rules 1996. Amend the tribunal rules concerned with equal-value cases to allow a tribunal to consider whether or not they need an independent expert's report when they are considering a case brought under the 'work of equal value' provisions. There are other modifications to the requirements concerning independent experts' reports, which are also intended to speed up the progress of equal-value claims.

38   Equal Pay Act 1970

Amended by Sex Discrimination Acts 1975 and 1986, Equal Pay (Amendment) Regulations 1983, Pensions Act 1995 Armed Forces Act 1996. The Employment Tribunals Rules of Procedure (Amendment) Rules 1996 (SI 1996 No. 1757) amend the procedure used to deal with equal-value claims.

38.1   Equality clause

The Act provides that a woman's contract is to have an equality clause implied into it if it does not specifically contain one. The effect of the equality clause is to modify the woman's contractual conditions so that they are no less favourable than those of a man who is engaged on like work or on work rated as equivalent.

38.2   The Equal Pay (Amendment) Regulations 1983

(a) These provide a new head under which parity may be claimed – where the man is on work of equal value to that of the woman. The effect of this amendment is threefold:
  (i) it has 'opened up a far wider field for claims than existed under the old law. Comparisons can now be made between totally dissimilar jobs, in different pay structures and across different collective bargaining groups'
  (ii) it allows for an independent expert to evaluate and compare jobs even where the employer has no job evaluation scheme in operation. (The Employment Tribunals Rules of Procedure (Amendment) Rules 1996 (SI 1996 No. 1757) amended the erstwhile requirement, brought in with the 1983 Regulations, that an independent expert must be appointed in equal-value cases. The 1996 amendments to the tribunal rules mean that the tribunal can now decide whether or not in the particular case an independent expert should be appointed. One of the difficulties in practice had been the length of time that such cases were taking due, in part, to the length of time taken to obtain independent experts' reports); and
  (iii) it allows an existing job evaluation scheme to be scrutinised by the tribunal to ensure that there is no discriminatory bias within the scheme itself.
(b) For equal-value claims the original material difference defence is amended to a material factor defence. (This, broadly, allows the employer to justify a difference on non-sex-based grounds – personal differences or market forces.)
(c) The Act and the amendments apply equally to men, who can, therefore, claim equality of terms with a woman on like work, work rated as equivalent, or on work of equal value.

39   European Communities Act 1972 – Treaty of Rome

The European Communities Act 1972 brought into effect the application of certain European regulations to UK law. Certain provisions of the Treaty of Rome are important in employment.

(a) Provisions allowing for free movement of labour across EC borders.
(b) Equal access for EC nationals to social security benefits.
(c) Equal pay. Article 119, which provides for 'equal pay for equal work', is wider than the Equal Pay Act 1970 and has direct effect in the UK.

40 Factories Act 1961

Amended by Sex Discrimination Act 1986 and Employment Act 1989, Manual Handling Operations Regulations 1992 (SI 1992/2793), Provision and Use of Work Equipment Regulations 1992 (SI 1992/2932), Workplace (Health, Safety and Welfare) Regulations 1992 (SI 1992/3004), Personal Protective Equipment at Work Regulations 1992 (SI 1992/2966), Education Act 1993, Health and Safety (Young Persons) Regulations 1997, Lifting Operations and Lifting Equipment Regulations 1998.

Consolidates previous Factories Acts of 1937, 1948 and 1959, establishes standards of health, safety and welfare in factories. It is intended, eventually, to bring all the health and safety provisions under the ambit of codes and regulations made under the Health and Safety at Work etc. Act 1974. The previous restrictions on the hours of work of women and young persons contained in the Factories Act were lifted by the Employment Act 1989.

41 Family Law Reform Act 1969

Reduced the age of majority from 21 to 18.

42 Finance Acts

The provisions of the Finance Acts, so far as they affect taxation of employment under Schedule 'E', are largely consolidated into the Income and Corporation Taxes Act 1988.

42.1 Finance Act 1989

Amends Income and Corporation Taxes Act 1988.
(a) Allows a tax exemption for those over 60 on payments made by them in respect of private medical insurance
(b) Increases the limits on 'payroll giving' schemes (charitable donations made directly from the payroll which are treated as a tax-free item) from £240 to £480.

42.2 Finance Act 1990

(a) Where an employer provides a 'workplace nursery', this benefit is no longer treated as a taxable benefit.
(b) Employees who use their private car for work may now claim a capital allowance for their car – ie some of the capital value of the car can be written off against the employee's Schedule E tax liability.

42.3 Finance Act 1991

Amended by Finance Act 1996.

(a) Mortgage interest relief, which could previously be set off against the whole of the employee's tax liability, can now only be set off against basic rate income tax. The maximum mortgage that qualifies for mortgage interest relief remains at £30,000.
(b) Employees who undertake vocational training which they pay for themselves qualify for income tax relief on the costs of the training from April 1992.
(c) From 1 January 1992 employers who have an 'executive share option scheme' are allowed to give participants up to 15 per cent discount on share prices provided that the company also operates a general share option scheme for all employees.
(d) From 1 January 1992 an investment of up to £3,000 may be made in a personal equity plan (PEP) in a single company in addition to the £6,000 investment which can be made in a general PEP. This is to encourage employee share ownership.
(e) Where an employer provides the employee with a portable telephone the employee has to pay tax on it on the basis of a new 'scale rate'.

42.4 Finance Act 1993

Amends Income and Corporation Taxes Act 1988.
(a) Sets out a new method of calculating the notional benefit of a company car and fuel provided for private use for the tax year 1994/95 onwards.
(b) Allows tax relief on the reasonable removal expenses reimbursed by an employer in respect of an employee moving to take up a new job or in cases where the employer moves or the employee's job is moved.

42.5 Finance Act 1996

Amends Taxes Act 1988, Finance Act 1991.
(a) Amends the vocational training reliefs in the Finance Act 1991.
(b) Amends the rules concerning the taxability of living accommodation provided for employees.

42.6 Finance Act 1997

Amends Taxes Act 1988.
(a) Phases out the profit-related pay reliefs so that the profit-related pay schemes cease to have effect from 1 January 2000.
(b) Allows an employee's travelling expenses to be deducted from his pay, for purposes of assessing the employee's Schedule E tax liability, to the extent that those expenses:
   • exceed his normal commuting expenses
   • are wholly, exclusively and necessarily expended in the performance of his duties; and
   • are not reimbursed to him.

43   Fire Precautions Act 1971

Amended by the Health and Safety at Work etc. Act 1974, Fire Safety and Safety of Places of Sport Act 1987 and by the Fire Precautions (Workplace) Regulations 1997.

Governs fire precautions in all places of work. The provisions governing fire precautions contained in the Factories Act 1961 and the Offices, Shops and Railway Premises Act 1963 are repealed.

43A   Fire Precautions (Workplace) Regulations 1997

Amend the Fire Precautions Act 1971 and Management of Health and Safety at Work Regulations 1992.

The onus for ensuring compliance with the Regulations in respect of the workplace is placed on employers.

(a) *Appropriate fire-fighting equipment*
   i)   The employer must ensure that the workplace is equipped with 'appropriate':
        ● fire-fighting equipment
        ● fire detectors; and
        ● alarms.
   ii) What equipment is 'appropriate' depends on:
        ● the dimensions of the building in which the workplace is situated
        ● the equipment it contains
        ● the physical and chemical properties of the substances likely to be present; and
        ● the maximum number of people that may be present at any one time.
   iii) Any non-automatic fire-fighting equipment must be:
        ● easily accessible
        ● simple to use; and
        ● indicated by signs.

(b) *Other measures*
   The employer must comply with as many of the following as necessary to safeguard his employees in case of fire:
   i)   taking measures for fire-fighting in the workplace adapted to:
        ● the nature of the activities carried on there
        ● the size of the undertaking
        ● the size of the workplace; and
        ● the number of people other than employees who may be present
   iii nominating sufficient employees to implement the measures taken and ensuring that the training and equipment with which they are provided is adequate having regard to the size of the workplace and the hazards involved
   iii) arranging any necessary contacts with external emergency services, particularly as regards rescue work and fire-fighting
   iv) providing emergency routes and exits:

- ensuring that they are kept clear
- ensuring that they lead as directly as possible to a safe place
- ensuring that emergency routes and exits are such that it is possible to evacuate the building quickly and safely, taking into account the number of people who may be present
- providing emergency doors which
  - open in the direction of escape
  - are not sliding or revolving doors
  - are not to be locked or fastened so they cannot be opened easily by anyone trying to escape
- ensuring that emergency routes and exits
  - are indicated by signs; and
  - have emergency illumination available if illumination is needed.

Failure to comply with these Regulations in such a way as to cause a serious risk (ie one where death or serious injury is likely to result) is a criminal offence. Fire authorities can also serve enforcement notices on employers who have failed to comply with their obligations under the Regulations.

44   Fire Safety and Safety of Places of Sport Act 1987

Amends Fire Precautions Act 1971 and Health and Safety at Work etc. Act 1974.

Tightens up on matters such as means of escape from premises in cases of fire and allows for improvement notices and prohibition notices to be served where an occupier of premises has inadequate provision either for escape in cases of fire, or for fire fighting.

45   Food Safety Act 1990

Gives local authorities powers to oversee company canteens to ensure food safety standards are met.

46   Further and Higher Education Act 1992

Amends Education Act 1944, Chronically Sick and Disabled Persons Act 1970, Sex Discrimination Act 1975, Race Relations Act 1976, Employment Act 1989.

Makes any provision in a contract of employment in the further education sector void insofar as it provides either:

- that the employee shall not be dismissed by reason of redundancy; or
- that if the employee is dismissed by reason of redundancy he shall receive a larger redundancy payment than would be payable under the ERA.

47   Health and Safety at Work etc. Act 1974

Amended by Sex Discrimination Act 1986, Fire Safety and Safety of Places of Sport

Act 1987, Employment Act 1989, Health and Safety (Young Persons) Regulations 1997, Police (Health and Safety) Act 1997, and Control of Substances Hazardous to Health Regulations 1999 (S1 1999 No 437).

It is ultimately intended to replace all existing safety legislation with regulations and codes of practice under this Act. To facilitate this transfer of jurisdiction, the Act absorbs the inspectorates provided for by a multitude of statutes dealing with safety matters (eg Factories Act 1961, Explosives Act 1875, Mines and Quarries Act 1954) into a single Health and Safety Executive which now deals with all such matters.

Part I of the Act has four purposes:
- securing the health, safety and welfare of persons at work
- protecting other persons against risks to health and safety arising out of, or in connection with, the activities of persons at work
- preventing the unlawful acquisition and possession of explosives and other highly flammable and dangerous substances and controlling their use and storage
- controlling the emission of noxious substances into the atmosphere.

These purposes are to be achieved to some extent by the Act itself which puts a general duty on employers, employees, the self-employed and other people who are concerned with the premises to have regard for the safety of others and themselves. Sections 15 and 16, respectively, provide for regulations to be made and for codes of practice. It should be noted that breaches of Part I of the Act give rise to criminal liability but not to civil liability, which is, therefore, largely the province of existing statutory and common law duties. Part II of the Act amends and repeals in part the Employment Medical Advisory Services Act 1972. Part III of the Act widens the scope of building regulations made under the Public Health Act 1936. (The Act amends and repeals parts of the Fire Precautions Act 1971, the Employment Medical Advisory Services Act 1972 and the Employment and Training Act 1973.)

48 Health and Safety (Consultation with Employees) Regulations 1996 (SI 1996 No. 1513)

Amends ERA and Safety Representatives and Safety Committees Regulations 1977 (SI 1977/500).

In 1994 the EC Commission successfully brought a case against the UK complaining of the UK's failure to implement the requirement for consultation in relation to collective redundancies and transfers of undertakings in cases where trade unions were not recognised. The HSCE Regulations are a spin-off of this in that the Framework Directive (Directive 89/391/EEC), articles 10 and 11, requires that there be consultation with employees on matters affecting health and safety. Until these regulations were brought in, the requirement for employers to consult with employees was restricted to employments in which trades unions were recognised (see Safety Representatives and Safety Committees Regulations 1977 (SI 1977/500)).

48.1 Exclusions

Employment in domestic households is excluded.

Where employees are represented by safety representatives under the Safety Representatives and Safety Committees Regulations 1977 SI 1977 No. 500 (SRSCR), the employer must consult with those safety representatives. Where there are no safety representatives the employer is required to consult under these regulations (cf. the Collective Redundancies and Transfer of Undertakings (Protection of Employment) (Amendment) Regulations 1995 SI 1995 No. 2587 where the employer has a choice as to whether to consult with a recognised trade union or with employee representatives).

48.2 Representatives of employee safety

Representatives of employee safety are elected by employees specifically to represent them on health and safety matters. They are entitled to paid time off for training, to carry out their functions and to stand for election. They are specifically protected from dismissal and action short of dismissal related to their functions under the ERA *(qv)*.

An employee representative's duties are:

- to make representations to the employer on general matters of health and safety and on potential hazards and dangerous occurrences at the workplace which affect, or could affect, the group of employees he represents; and
- to represent the group of employees he represents in consultations at the workplace with health and safety inspectors.

48.3 Consultation

(a) *With whom*

   The employer must consult either employees who are affected or representatives of employee safety who have been elected by the group of employees in question to represent them.

(b) *About what*

The employer must consult in good time on matters regarding employees' health and safety at work, in particular on
   - the introduction of:
     - measures which may substantially affect employees' health and safety; and
     - new technology
   - arrangements for:
     - appointing people to be responsible for statutory health and safety duties
     - nominating people to deal with serious and imminent dangers at work and danger areas
   - health and safety information which he is required to provide by statute
   - planning of health and safety training he is required to provide by statute.

(c) *Requirement to provide information*

The employer must provide information for the employees or their representatives to have all relevant information which he has available which will allow them to participate fully and effectively in consultation. Certain types of confidential information are excluded from this requirement.

49 Health and Safety (Display Screen Equipment) Regulations 1992 (SI 1992 No. 2792)

This is one of the 'Six-pack' Regulations introduced in 1992 arising from European health and safety directives.

(a) *Display screen users*

The requirements of these regulations are limited to 'display screen users', ie those to whom all or most of the following criteria apply:

(i)   the employee requires display screen equipment (DSE) to do the job – other means are not readily available

(ii) the employee has no discretion as to whether or not to use DSE

(iii) the employee requires training in the use of DSE to do the job

(iv) the employee normally uses DSE for continuous periods of an hour or more

(v)   the employee uses DSE in this way more or less daily

(vi) fast transfer of information between the user and the screen is an important requirement of the job

(vii) performance requirements demand high levels of attention and concentration by the user – eg where the consequences of error may be critical.

(b) *Work stations for DSE users*

(i)   Work stations used by DSE users must be assessed for risks and reassessed if there has been a significant change. The matters that need to be looked at range from the equipment itself (including the software) and the desk and chair the user will use, to the surroundings in which they will use it – including consideration of matters such as glare and reflection on the screen, ambient noise, heat from equipment, etc.

(ii) By December 1996 all work stations were required to meet a specification laid down in the schedule to the Display Screen Equipment Regulations.

(c) *Daily work routine of DSE users*

(i)   The job of DSE users should be so designed as to ensure that they have regular breaks or changes in activity to reduce their workload on the equipment.

(ii) This may be done by:
  ● job design – putting natural breaks into the work itself; or
  ● providing for specific breaks (such breaks should be taken away from the screen where possible).

(d) *Eye tests*

(i)   Regular professional eye tests must be provided by the employer for DSE users at the employer's expense

   (ii)   If there is a specific visual difficulty which may reasonably be considered to be caused by work on DSE the employer must provide a further eye test if the employee so wishes.

   (iii) The employer must provide spectacles where they are needed specifically for DSE work (but not if the problem with using DSE would be overcome by using spectacles which the person requires for normal use).

(e) *Health and safety training*

   (i)   The employer must ensure that DSE users are trained in health and safety aspects of DSE.

   (ii)   The employer must ensure that DSE users are retrained in health and safety if their work station is modified significantly.

(f) *Health and safety information*

   (i)   Employers must provide DSE users with information on all aspects of health and safety re DSE work stations.

   (ii)   Employers must provide DSE users with information on measures taken by them to comply with:

- the requirement to give breaks to DSE users
- the requirement to give health and safety training to DSE users
- the availability of eye testing and specialised spectacles where these are required.

49A   The Health and Safety (Young Persons) Regulations 1997 (SI 1997 No. 135)

Amend the Management of Health and Safety at Work Regulations 1992, Factories Act 1961 and Offices Shops and Railway Premises Act 1963. These Regulations are made to give effect to Articles 6 and 7 of the EC Directive on the Protection of Young People at Work (94/33/EC)

(a) *Defines 'young person' for purposes of the Management of Health and Safety at Work Regulations 1992*

'Young person' is defined as anyone who has not attained the age of 18.

(b) *Disapplies the Management of Health and Safety at Work Regulations 1992 to certain categories*

   i)   those employed on sea-going ships

   ii) those engaged on short-term or occasional work in:

- domestic service in a private household; or
- a family undertaking where the work is not harmful, damaging or dangerous to young people

(c) *Requires an assessment of risks to young persons*

Other than in the cases where the Regulations are disapplied (see (b) above) any employer must make a risk assessment in relation to the health and safety of any young person/s employed by him, having particular regard to:

   i)   the inexperience, lack of awareness of risks and immaturity of young persons

   ii) the fitting-out and layout of the workplace and the workstation

    iii)   the nature, degree and duration of the exposure to physical, biological and chemical agents

    iv)   the form, range and use of work equipment and the way in which it is handled

    v)   the organisation of processes and activities

    vi)   the extent of the health and safety training which is provided to young persons

    vii)   risks from agents, processes and types of work listed in the Annex to Council Directive 94/33/EC

(d) *Requires employers to provide comprehensible and relevant information to the parents of any child they employ on*:

    i)   the risks to the child's health and safety identified by the assessment

    ii)   the preventive and protective measures taken; and

    iii)   the risks arising from another employer in a shared workplace

(e) *Imposes a series of duties on employers in terms of the protection of young persons*

    i)   employers have a general duty to ensure that young persons are protected from risks to their health and safety which are a consequence of inexperience, lack of awareness of risks or immaturity

    ii)   an employer, having considered the risk assessment, may not employ a young person for work:

- beyond his physical or physiological capabilities
- which may in any way chronically affect human health
- involving harmful radiation
- involving risk of accidents which it may reasonably be assumed cannot be recognised or avoided by young persons because of insufficient attention to safety, or lack of experience or training; or
- where there is a risk to health from:
  - extremes of temperature
  - noise; or
  - vibration

    iii)   these restrictions do not apply where:

- the person employed is no longer a child (ie is above school leaving age)
- the work is necessary for his training
- he will be supervised by a competent person; and
- the risk has been reduced to the lowest level that is reasonably practicable.

50 Health and Social Security Act 1984 (largely repealed)

Amends Social Security Pensions Act 1975 and Social Security and Housing Benefits Act 1982.

Amended by Social Security Act 1985 and Wages Act 1986, is now largely repealed by the Social Security (Consequential Provisions) Act 1992.

50A   Human Rights Act 1998

Provides a fundamental set of human rights to give effect to the European Convention on Human Rights.

Most important of the rights provided for, in employment terms, is:
Freedom of assembly and association
- the right includes:
  - right of peaceful assembly
  - the freedom to associate with others, including the right to form and join trade unions
- restrictions can be placed on these rights by law only
  - in the interests of public security and safety
  - for the prevention of crime
  - for the protection of the rights and freedoms of others

51   Immigration Act 1971

Amends and replaces previous immigration laws. Is amended by the Asylum and Immigration Act 1996.

Generally, except for certain occupations such as dentistry and medicine, any non-patrials require work permits to work in the UK. The provisions of the Act have now been amended to allow EC nationals to take up employment in the UK freely.

52   Income and Corporation Taxes Act 1988

Consolidates much of the earlier legislation concerning taxation of income and other benefits arising from employment.

Amended by Finance Acts 1989, 1993, 1996 and 1997, Police Act 1997.

53   Industrial Training Act 1964

Repealed by Industrial Training Act 1982 and Agricultural Training Board Act 1982 except for s 16 allowing local education authorities to provide vocational training.

54   Industrial Tribunals Act 1996 (renamed the Employment Tribunals Act 1996 *qv*)

55   Industrial Tribunals Extension of Jurisdiction (England and Wales) Order 1994 (SI 1994/1623)/(Scotland – SI 1994/1624) (renamed Employment Tribunals Extension of Jurisdiction (England and Wales) Order 1994 *qv*)

56   Industrial Tribunals Rules of Procedure (Amendment) Rules 1996 (SI 1996 No. 1757) (renamed Employment Tribunals Rules of Procedure (Amendment) Rules 1996 *qv*)

57   Industrial Training Act 1982

Amended by Employment Act 1989.

Consolidates the law relating to industrial training boards.

58   Industry Acts 1975 and 1980

The 1975 Act is amended by the Industry Act 1980.

The 1980 Act removes much of the ambit and effect of the 1975 Act. The National Enterprise Board (NEB) is retained but those parts of the Act dealing with disclosure of information to the government and to trade unions are repealed.

The remaining objectives of the NEB are:

(a) to promote the efficiency and international competitiveness of British industry
(b) to provide and protect productive employment; and
(c) to prevent important firms from coming under unacceptable foreign ownership.

59   Industry Act 1981

Amends the financial limits imposed on the NEB by earlier Acts and gives the Secretary of State for Employment power to make grants or loans to anybody:

(a) to promote the practice of engineering
(b) to encourage and improve links between industry and educational courses; and
(c) to encourage young persons and others to take up careers in industry and to follow appropriate educational courses.

60   Insolvency Act 1985

Amended Employment Protection (Consolidation) Act 1978. This amendment is now consolidated into ERA.

Replaced s 122(4) EPCA with a new subsection setting out certain items which are to be treated as items of arrears of pay for purposes of s 122 (see also Insolvency Act 1986 below). These are:

(a) guarantee payment
(b) remuneration from suspension on medical grounds
(c) payment in respect of statutory time-off; and
(d) payment under a protective award.

This is now consolidated into s 184(2) Employment Rights Act 1996.

61   Insolvency Act 1986

Amends Employment Protection (Consolidation) Act 1978.

Certain employee debts are given priority over other debts:

(a) remuneration for up to eight weeks preceding the date when the employer became insolvent up to a statutory maximum
(b) where an employee's employment was terminated before the employer became insolvent, then arrears of holiday pay of up to six weeks can be recouped.

62   Job Release Act 1977

Provides for early retirement for those approaching pension age for purposes of making work available for the unemployed or otherwise for mitigating the effects of high unemployment.

63   Jobseekers Act 1995

Amends the Social Security Contributions and Benefits Act 1992, Social Security Administration Act 1992, Social Security (Incapacity for Work) Act 1994.

This Act was passed to replace Unemployment Benefit with a new Jobseeker's Allowance.

63.1   Statutory exclusions from entitlement

(a) *Trade dispute*

An employee who is unemployed either because he is taking part in a trade dispute or because he has a direct interest in it is disqualified from entitlement to Jobseeker's Allowance. He will be qualified to receive Jobseeker's Allowance again if, during the trade dispute:

(i)   he becomes *bona fide* employed elsewhere

(ii)   his employment is terminated by reason of redundancy; or

(iii)   he has *bona fide* resumed employment with his employer, but has subsequently left for a reason other than the trade dispute.

(b) *Misconduct and voluntary leaving*

An employee can be disqualified from entitlement to Jobseeker's Allowance for up to 26 weeks if he:

● loses his employment through misconduct; or

● voluntarily leaves employment without just cause.

For these purposes a person who is dismissed for redundancy, after having volunteered for redundancy, is to be considered not to have left voluntarily.

(c) *Reduction for pension payments*

The Act provides that regulations can be made to take into account the amount of any personal or occupational pension which an individual is entitled to in determining the amount of Jobseeker's Allowance that is payable. Under the previous law, pension payments were taken into account in ascertaining an individual's entitlement to unemployment benefit if that individual was over 55 years old.

63A   The Lifting Operations and Lifting Equipment Regulations 1998 (SI 1998 No. 2307)

Amend the Factories Act 1961. These Regulations are made to give effect, as respects lifting equipment, to the Council Directive on Minimum Health and Safety Requirements for the Use of Work Equipment by Workers at Work (89/655/EEC as amended by 95/63/EC)

The Regulations make provisions concerning the strength, stability, safety, installation, marking, inspecting and use of lifting equipment at work.

64   Local Government Act 1988

Restricts Local Authorities from having regard to 'non-commercial' considerations when awarding public supply or works contracts. Such non-commercial considerations include:

(a) terms and conditions of employment afforded by contractors to their employees

(b) composition of the workforce, and arrangements for promotion, transfer or training of the workforce – ie discrimination consideration.

   (While considerations of discrimination by a contractor on grounds of race may be looked at as a relevant factor by an authority when considering whether or not to award a contract to a contractor, considerations of sex discrimination may not be taken into account.)

   'Contract compliance' – ie forcing contractors to have non-discriminatory policies and terms and conditions of employment which are as good as the local levels – is, in a general sense, outlawed by this provision.

(c) whether the contractor's workers are employed or self-employed

(d) conduct of contractors or workers in any industrial disputes

(e) any interests a contractor may have in any other country

(f) any political affiliation or activities of the contractor.

65   Local Government and Housing Act 1989

Amended by Disability Discrimination Act 1995.

   Prevents senior local authority staff from becoming members of any local housing authority.

66   Management of Health and Safety at Work Regulations (SI 1992 No. 2051)

Amended by The Health and Safety (Young Persons) Regulations 1997, Fire Precautions (Workplace) Regulations 1997.

This is one of the 'Six-pack' Regulations introduced in 1992 arising from European health and safety directives.

   The Regulations amend Safety Representatives and Safety Committees Regulations 1977 (SI 1977 No. 500), Offices, Shops and Railway Premises Act 1963 and Factories Act 1961.

(a) *Risk assessment*

   (i) The Regulations require an employer to make a suitable and sufficient assessment of

   • risks to the health and safety of employees at work; and

   • risks to the health and safety of others who are affected by the conduct of his undertaking

   so that appropriate protective and preventive measures which need to be taken to comply with any statutory provision can be identified. This includes measures which need to be taken under Control of Substances

　　　　Hazardous to Health Regulations 1988 as well as the more general health and safety requirements under HASWA and the other 'six-pack' directives, etc.

(ii)　The employer must also identify:
   - significant findings of the assessment that is made; and
   - any groups of employees assessed as being at special risk

　　　　and record these findings in writing.

(iii)　The risk assessment must be reviewed if:
   - there is reason to suspect that it is no longer valid; or
   - there has been a significant change in the matters to which it relates.

(iv)　Where a number of employers share a workplace they must co-operate in fulfilling their statutory health and safety duties. They should also take all reasonable steps to co-ordinate their health and safety efforts and they must provide each other with information about the risks to the other employer's employees arising from their operations.

(b) *Health and safety arrangements*

(i)　The Regulations require employers to make and put into effect appropriate arrangements, having regard to the nature of their activities and the size of the undertaking, for the effective planning, organisation, control, monitoring and review of the preventive and protective measures shown by the risk assessment to be necessary. This requirement is aimed at having some sort of system for the ongoing monitoring and review of health and safety measures in the workplace.

(ii)　Where the employer employs more than five people these arrangements must also be recorded in writing.

(c) *Health surveillance*

Employers are required to ensure that employees are provided with such health surveillance as is appropriate having regard to the risks to their health and safety which are identified by the risk assessment which has been carried out. If a particular type of operation could potentially have an adverse effect on an employee's health, then the employer must assess the employee's health on an ongoing basis.

　　The type of health surveillance that would apply in the majority of employments is exemplified by providing eyesight tests for those using VDUs.

(d) *Health and safety assistance*

(i)　Employers must appoint one or more competent persons to assist in undertaking the measures they need to take to comply with the various statutory health and safety provisions. Where more than one person is appointed the employer must ensure that they all co-operate with each other.

(ii)　The employer is required to consult with the appropriate people or the appropriate body about the appointment of his assistant under this provision. The appropriate people or bodies are:
   - where a trade union is recognised, safety representatives under Safety

Representatives and Safety Committees Regulations 1977 (SI 1977 No. 500)

- where no trade union is recognised, then either the employees themselves or representatives of employee safety appointed under Health and Safety (Consultation with Employees) Regulations 1996 (SI 1996 No. 1513).

(e) *Procedures for serious and imminent danger and for danger areas*
  (i) Employers need to establish and where necessary give effect to appropriate procedures to be followed in the event of serious and imminent danger to employees. This includes procedures for:
    - making sure that those who are exposed to serious and imminent danger are informed:
      - of the nature of the hazard; and
      - of the steps taken or to be taken to protect them from it
    - enabling people to stop work and go to a safe place in the event of serious, imminent and unavoidable danger
    - preventing people from returning to work while a serious and imminent danger continues.
  (ii) Employers must nominate sufficient competent people to implement any evacuation procedures. Safety representatives, employees or representatives of employee safety must be consulted about these nominations (as per (d)(ii) above). The most obvious situation to which this applies is evacuation in the case of fire or bomb threat.
  (iii) Employers must also ensure that no employee has access to an area to which access is restricted on health and safety grounds unless that employee has received adequate health and safety training.

(f) *Information for employees*
  Employers must give employees comprehensible and relevant information on:
  - risks to their health and safety identified by the risk assessment
  - preventive and protective measures taken following the assessment
  - the procedures to be followed by the employees in cases of serious and imminent danger – in most cases this will entail having at least a set fire evacuation procedure
  - any risks to employees arising out of the operations of another employer who shares premises with the employer.

(g) *Employees' duties and training*
  (i) Employers must take into account an employee's capabilities to do a task, in health and safety terms, before entrusting that task to that employee.
  (ii) Employers must also ensure that employees are provided with adequate health and safety training during working hours:
    - when they are recruited
    - when they are exposed to new or increased risks because of:
      - a transfer or change of responsibility

- the introduction of a new system of work, new machinery or new technology
- a change in the system of work or in the way in which existing machinery is used.

(iii) Employees must use any health and safety equipment provided to them by their employer, including machinery, materials and safety equipment, in accordance with any training and instruction given by the employer.

(iv) Employees must inform their employer or a fellow employee with health and safety responsibility of any situation or matter that affects them or their work:

- which they reasonably consider to be a serious and imminent danger to health and safety; or
- which they reasonably consider to be a shortcoming in the employer's arrangements for health and safety protection.

This duty on an employee is limited to what his training and experience would make him realise was a serious risk or a shortcoming in health and safety arrangements.

67   Manual Handling Operations Regulations 1992 (SI 1992 No. 2793)

This is one of the 'Six-pack' Regulations introduced in 1992 arising from European health and safety directives.

The Regulations amend the Offices, Shops and Railway Premises Act 1963 and the Factories Act 1961.

(a) Manual handling is concerned with moving objects around usually by lifting, but also by pushing or pulling.

(b) Manual handling which shows in the general risk assessment as potentially involving risk of injury should be avoided if possible.

(c) If manual handling cannot be avoided, it should be automated as far as is practicable.

(d) Where it is not possible to avoid manual handling, an assessment must be made of all manual handling which is necessary and which involves a risk of injury. The assessment needs to be repeated if it gets out of date.

(e) Steps must be taken to reduce the risk to employees to the lowest possible level, including:

- increasing automation
- reducing weights to be carried
- putting the weights into smaller packages
- making the packages more manageable
- redesigning the workplace or the job where the lifting is carried out to minimise risks.

(f) Employers must also provide guidance on:

- lifting techniques
- the weight of each load; and

- where the centre of gravity of a load is not central, on which side the load is heaviest.

67A National Minimum Wage Act 1998 and National Minimum Wage Regulations 1999 (SI 1999 No. 584)

The Act amends the Agricultural Wages Act 1948, Employment Tribunals Act 1996 and Employment Rights Act 1996.

Amended by the Employment Relations Act 1999.

The Act establishes a framework for the national minimum wage, which took effect from April 1999. Much of the substance concerning those who are not entitled to receive the national minimum wage, the rate of the national minimum wage, the times of work in respect of which it is payable, remuneration to be set off against it and record keeping are dealt with by the National Minimum Wage Regulations 1999. In this commentary no distinction is made between provisions arising directly under the Act and those provided by the Regulations.

(a) *Who is entitled?*

i)   A person is entitled to the national minimum wage if he:
- is a worker
- is working or ordinarily works in the UK under his contract
- is over 18

ii)   a worker means
- a person who has entered into or works under a contract of employment
- a person who works under a contract of apprenticeship
- someone who is under a contract to perform work personally for the employer where the employer is not a customer or client of that person's business

iii)   a worker also includes
- someone who works through an employment agency – even if there is no contract directly between the company and the worker (the person who is liable to pay the national minimum wage is whoever is liable to pay the worker's pay)
- homeworkers, even if they are not under a contract to perform the work personally
- mariners, but not share fishermen, employed on UK-registered ships unless:
  - all their duties are performed outside the UK; and
  - they are not resident in the UK

People in offshore employment are included by The National Minimum Wage (Offshore Employment) Order 1999.

The Secretary of State has the power to add to those to whom the Act applies.

iv)   Those excluded from entitlement to the national minimum wage include:

- voluntary workers who are not paid or otherwise remunerated for their work (the Employment Relations Act 1999 also excludes those who are part of a resident religious community)
- prisoners in respect of work done under the prison rules
- those in the armed forces
- a person who lives in the employer's household and who is either a member of that household or who is treated as a member of that household is excluded from entitlement to the national minimum wage for:
  - household work; or
  - work in running the family business
- a worker who is under 26 and who is employed on a contract of apprenticeship or on a modern apprenticeship who is:
  - in the first year of employment (including any period of continuous employment); or
  - who has not attained the age of 19
- a worker who is on a Government scheme designed to provide him with training, work experience or temporary work which is funded in part or wholly under the European Social Fund
- a worker who is working as part of a first degree course or initial teacher training
- a homeless person who is provided with shelter and other benefits for performing work
- those who are members of residential religious communities (from 25 October 1999).

(b) *Who is liable to pay?*
  i)   Normally the employer is liable to pay the minimum wage.
  ii) Where a worker is employed by someone who is himself employed by an employer and the worker works on the superior employer's premises, then both the worker's immediate employer and the superior employer are considered to be the worker's employer for purposes of the Act.

(c) *The national minimum wage*
  i)   The national minimum wage is a single hourly rate and is prescribed by the Secretary of State, after consultation with the Low Pay Commission.
  ii) A lower rate of national minimum wage is set for those who are between 18 and 22.
  iii) A rate between the above two rates is set for those who are:
    - over 22.
    - in the first six months of continuous employment with their employer; and
    - required to take part in accredited training on at least 26 days in the first six months of that contract.

(d) *Items that can and cannot be set off against the employer's liability to pay the national minimum wage*

i) The following can be set off against the employer's liability
- any contractual remuneration
- any payments made under the Agricultural Wages Act

ii) The following cannot be set off against the employer's liability
- benefits in kind, other than living accommodation, which can be set off at a very low fixed rate.
- vouchers or stamps which can be exchanged for goods, services or money
- any loan or advance of wages
- pension or compensation for loss of office
- redundancy payment
- any award of a court or payment in settlement of a matter which was or could have been taken to court by the worker
- any payment made under a suggestion scheme

(e) *Calculating the worker's entitlement*

i) The worker's entitlement is calculated over a reference period of a month, or a lower period if the worker is paid more frequently

ii) There are complex provisions for calculating an employee's entitlement depending on his working regime, contained in the National Minimum Wage Regulations 1999

(f) *Records*

i) Records of payments
- The employer must keep records which are sufficient to show that he is remunerating the worker at a rate at least equal to the national minimum wage.

ii) Worker's right of access to records
- Where the worker believes, on reasonable grounds, that he has been or is being remunerated at less than the national minimum wage he can serve a 'production' notice on his employer requiring production of any relevant statutory national minimum wage records for the relevant period.
- The employer must then give the employee reasonable notice of when and where the records will be produced.
- The records must be produced:
  - at the worker's place of work
  - at such other place as is reasonable in all the circumstances; or
  - at a place agreed between the employer and the employee.
- The records must be produced within 14 days of the production notice or such later time as is agreed between the employer and the worker during the 14-day period.
- The worker is entitled to be accompanied at an inspection by 'such other person as the worker may think fit'.
- If the employer fails to produce the relevant records or fails to allow the

worker to exercise any of his rights, a complaint may be made to an employment tribunal within three months of:
- the end of the 14-day period; or
- the agreed production date if that was to be later; or
- if it is not reasonably practicable for the employee's claim to be presented within these time limits, within such further period as the tribunal considers reasonable.
- If the tribunal finds the claim to be valid it shall:
  - make a declaration to that effect; and
  - award 80 times the hourly national minimum wage.

(g) *Officers may be appointed under the Act*

  i)   Officers' powers of inspection. An officer can require a 'relevant person' to allow him to:
- inspect relevant records
- require an explanation of any relevant records; and
- enter on to premises to carry out the above.

  ii)   A 'relevant person' for these purpose is:
- the worker's employer
- an employment agent through or for whom the worker is working
- a person who supplies work to an individual who qualifies for the national minimum wage
- any employee or agent of any of the above; or
- anyone who qualifies for the national minimum wage.

  iii)   Enforcement and penalty notices

If an officer is of opinion that a worker has been remunerated at a rate which is less than the national minimum wage for any period he can serve the employer with an enforcement notice requiring the employer to pay the difference.

The employer can appeal to an employment tribunal against an enforcement notice within four weeks of the notice

If an enforcement notice is not complied with, the officer can:
- sue on behalf of the employee/s covered by the enforcement notice
  - either at an employment tribunal – under the protection of wages provisions; or
  - in the civil court as a breach of contract
- serve the employer with a penalty notice which states:
  - the amount of the fixed penalty (including the calculation of the fixed penalty) – the amount is currently set at twice the hourly national minimum wage per worker to whom the failure to comply relates per day of non-compliance
  - the time within which the financial penalty is to be paid (which must be not less than four weeks from service of the notice – it should be noted that the fact that an employer has appealed against an enforcement notice does not prevent a penalty notice from being

served, although the employer need not comply with it until the appeal has been decided)
- the period to which the financial penalty relates
- the respects in which the officer considers that the enforcement notice has not be complied with; and
- the calculation of the amount of the financial penalty

The employer can appeal against the penalty notice.

h) *Enforcing the right to national minimum wage*
- i) A worker can claim any deficiency in pay below the national minimum wage under the protection of wages part of the Employment Rights Act 1996 (ERA).
- ii) Workers who are entitled to the national minimum wage, but who are not generally covered by the protection of the ERA, are given a specific right to be treated as if they were covered by the ERA for purposes of making a claim.

(i) *Right not to suffer a detriment or to be unfairly dismissed*
- i) A worker is entitled not to be dismissed, or to suffer a detriment by any act or deliberate failure by his employer to act, on grounds:
  - that any action was, or was proposed to be, taken by or on behalf of any worker to secure any benefit or right under the legislation
  - of any action taken in prosecuting the employer for an offence under the Act
  - of any action taken because the worker will qualify for national minimum wage or for a different rate of national minimum wage.
- ii) There is no qualifying period for the right to bring a claim of unfair dismissal on these grounds.

(j) *Reversal of the burden of proof in civil proceedings*
- i) it is presumed that the claimant qualifies for the national minimum wage; and
- ii) that the worker was paid at less than the national minimum wage
  unless, in either case, the contrary is proved.

(k) *Contracting out*
- i) the normal rules against contracting out apply
- ii) however, a settlement can be reached
  - through ACAS; or
  - through a compromise agreement.

(l) *Offences under the Act*
- i) refusal or deliberate neglect to pay a worker the national minimum wage
- ii) failure to keep any record required to be kept under the Act
- iii) producing a record with inaccurate information
- iv) delaying or obstructing an officer in exercise of his duties under the Act
- v) refusing to answer any question asked by an officer or to produce any document asked for by him.

It is a defence to any such charge to show that the person charged exercised all due diligence and took all reasonable precautions to secure that the rquirements of the legislation were complied with by himself and any person under his control.

Where an offence is by a body corporate then any director, manager or secretary who has consented to or connived in the offence is made personally liable.

68   Oil and Gas (Enterprise) Act 1982

The Oil and Gas (Enterprise) Act 1982 contains provisions repealing the extensions of the sex and race discrimination legislation contained in the Employment (Continental Shelf) Act 1978. An Order will need to be made under the 1982 Act to give effect to these repeals.

69   Offices, Shops and Railway Premises Act 1963

Amended by Fire Precautions Act 1971, Health and Safety at Work etc. Act 1974, Manual Handling Operations Regulations 1992 (SI 1992/2793), Provision and Use of Work Equipment Regulations 1992 (SI 1992/2932) and Workplace (Health, Safety and Welfare) Regulations 1992 (SI 1992/3004), Health and Safety (Young Persons) Regulations 1997, Police Act 1997.

The purpose of this Act was to establish a code of safety and welfare for those places of work not covered by the then existing legislation. It is concerned largely with welfare provisions such as adequate ventilation, light, warmth and washing facilities (much of which is now covered by Regulations). Fire precautions in premises subject to this statute are now covered by the 1971 Act as amended.

70   Patents Act 1977

Amended by Copyright, Design and Patents Act 1988.

Provides a method of determining the ownership, as between employer and employee, of an employee's inventions and also provides for the employee to be given compensation for his invention in certain circumstances. The invention will belong to the employer if:

(a) it was made in the course of either the employee's normal duties or special duties that had been assigned to him; and in either case an invention was, in the circumstances, to be reasonably expected from his carrying out these duties; or

(b) the employee made the invention in the course of his duties and because of the nature of his duties and the particular responsibilities arising from the nature of those duties he was under a special obligation to further his employer's interests. In all other cases the invention belongs to the employee.

An application for compensation for an invention may be made to the Comptroller or Patents Court:

(i)   if the invention belongs to the employer under the Act; and it has been patented; and it is of outstanding benefit to the employer; or

(ii)   where the patented invention belongs to the employee and has been assigned to the employer or the employer has been granted an exclusive licence to the invention by the employee; and the benefit derived by the employee is inadequate in relation to the benefit derived from the patent by the employer.

The amount of compensation, in either case, is to be a 'fair share' of the benefit that the employer has derived from the patent.

71   Payment of Wages Act 1960 (repealed)

Repealed by Wages Act 1986.

72   Pensions Act 1995

Amends the Equal Pay Act 1970, Sex Discrimination Act 1975, EPCA, Companies Acts 1985 and 1989, Insolvency Act 1986, Social Security Act 1989, SSBCA, Pensions Schemes Act 1993, and various other Acts in connection with the equalisation of State pension age.

Amended by the ERA.

72.1   General regulation of occupational pension schemes

(a) The Act sets up a closer regulatory system to ensure the security of employees' pensions. It introduces the Occupational Pensions Regulatory Authority which has power to remove trustees of a pension scheme or to suspend them. The OPRA can also appoint trustees to replace any it removes. The OPRA's powers extend to winding up a pension scheme if it considers that that is necessary to protect the interests of the generality of the members of the scheme.

(b) There are restrictions on employer-related investments and on employers taking the benefit of any surplus in the scheme, as well as minimum funding requirements for 'final salary' schemes. A provision, waiting to be brought into effect by statutory Order will make it an offence for an employer not to pay over to the pension scheme any pension contributions deducted from employees.

(c) The OPRA's inspectors are given powers to enter on to premises for purposes of investigating whether the regulatory provisions applicable to an occupational pension scheme have been complied with. The powers are in much the same terms as the powers that social security inspectors are given in relation to social security inspections under the Social Security Administration Act 1992 (see below).

(d) A minimum number of trustees are required to be nominated by members of the scheme and the Act requires an independent trustee to be appointed in certain circumstances. There are also provisions for employee trustees to be appointed.

(e) A statutory Order may be made bringing into effect provisions under which trustees will be required to increase the value of pensions under the scheme by the rise in the cost of living index or 5 per cent (whichever is the lower). This will not apply to any part of the pension stemming from additional voluntary contributions.

(f) The Act introduces the Pensions Compensation Board, which can make compensation payments to the trustees of a trust scheme if the employer is insolvent and if the value of the assets of the scheme has been reduced unlawfully to a level of 90 per cent or less of the liabilities of the scheme.

(g) The powers of the Pensions Ombudsman are prospectively extended by the Act.

72.2   Employee trustees

The provisions for paid time off and training for employee pension scheme trustees are now contained in the ERA (*qv*).

72.3   Equalisation of state pensionable age

State pensionable age is increased for women born after 6 April 1950. There is a gradual increase, over a 10-year period, so that pension age will ultimately be equalised at 65 for all those born after 6 April 1955.

72.4   Equal treatment in relation to occupational pension schemes

Provision for equal treatment in relation to occupational pension schemes was originally introduced by Schedule 5 Social Security Act 1989. These provisions were enacted to give effect to EC Directive 86/378/EEC on the equal treatment for men and women in relation to occupational social security schemes. Following the ECJ's judgment in *Barber* v *Guardian Royal Exchange Assurance Group* [1990] IRLR 240 it became clear that equal treatment under occupational pension schemes from 17 May 1990, the date of the ECJ's judgment in Barber, had to be treated as a matter of equal pay. The provisions of this Act, therefore, overtook the provisions of the Social Security Act 1989, as far as pensions were concerned. The Act adopts a framework for equal treatment in relation to occupational pension schemes which closely mirrors the provisions of the Equal Pay Act 1970. These provisions are applicable to pensionable service on or after 17 May 1990.

(a) *The equal treatment rule*

The equal treatment rule relates to the terms on which people become members of the scheme and to the terms on which members of pension schemes are treated. This includes:

- *Discretionary matters*: Trustees or managers of pension schemes are often given discretionary powers under the scheme. The Act provides that where there is any discretionary power that could be exercised in a way that is detrimental to a woman, then the effect of the equal treatment rule is to bar the trustees from exercising their discretion in that way.
- *Dependants' benefits*: Where the scheme provides benefits for dependants of members (for example, life assurance cover or survivor's pensions) then these too are subject to the requirement of equal treatment between scheme members.

All occupational pension schemes that do not specifically contain an equal treatment rule are deemed to include one. Where the rules of the scheme do not allow for the scheme to be altered to accommodate the requirements of an equal treatment rule, the trustees are given the power to alter the scheme by resolution to accommodate the equal treatment rule and its effects. Any such alteration can be retrospective.

(b) *Who can claim?*

Those who are on 'like work', 'work rated as equivalent' or engaged on 'work of equal value' to:

- a comparator of the opposite sex; or
- a comparator of the opposite sex and of the same marital status (where benefits differ with marital status)

are entitled to have any term of the scheme which is unfavourable to them modified so as to be as favourable to them as it is to their comparator.

(c) *Exclusions*

- *Material difference*: As with equal pay, there is an exclusion where the trustees of the scheme can show that the differences in the terms or effects of the scheme are due to a material difference between the two employees other than the difference in their sex.
- *Maternity and family leave*: The equal treatment rule for pensions is subject to the equality provisions in the Social Security Act 1989 relating to maternity and family leave.
- *State pension*: A difference in treatment is allowed, in pension schemes, if that difference arises purely out of the difference in entitlement to a State retirement pension between the sexes.
- *Actuarial calculations*: A difference in treatment is allowed if it is the result of a difference in actuarial calculations for each sex in respect of:
  - the level of the employer's contributions to the scheme; or
  - the level of benefit from the scheme.

(d) *Claims*

The equal treatment rule is treated as one with the requirement for equal treatment in relation to pay under the Equal Pay Act 1970 and a case may be brought to an employment tribunal in the same way.

To be entitled to claim, the employee must bring a claim within six months of the time when he or she was employed in a category of job to which the pension scheme in question applied.

The Sex Discrimination Act 1975 is amended to include, within the definition of grounds on which it is unlawful to victimise an employee, the fact that a person has made a claim under these provisions.

73 Pension Schemes Act 1993

Amends the Social Security Act 1973, Social Security Pensions Act 1975, EPCA, Social Security Act 1979, Social Security Act 1980, Social Security Act 1981, Social Security and Housing Benefits Act 1982, Health and Social Security Act 1984, Insolvency Act 1985, Insolvency Act 1986, Social Security Act 1986, Social Security

Act 1988, Social Security Act 1989, Employment Act 1989, Social Security Act 1990, TULRA, Social Security Act 1993.

Amended by the Pensions Act 1995.

This Act was passed to consolidate and amend some of the law relating to pension schemes.

73.1 'Contracted-out pension schemes'

The Act contains the definition of 'contracted-out employment' for pension purposes. Contracted-out pension schemes are those which are contracted out of the earnings-related part of the State scheme. To be contracted out pension schemes need to meet the appropriate requirements of the Act.

73.2 Reclaiming unpaid pension deductions

The Act deals with the case where an employer becomes insolvent after an employee has had deductions made from pay for pension scheme contributions. In such cases, if any such contributions have not been paid to the pension scheme, someone acting on behalf of a pension scheme can apply to the Secretary of State for payments to be made equivalent to any such sums. If the Secretary of State fails to pay then a person acting for the pension scheme can apply to an employment tribunal to order those payments to be made. Outstanding contributions to an employer's pension scheme are given priority in the event of the employer's bankruptcy to the extent that those contributions relate to the 12 months prior to insolvency.

73.3 Individuals' rights in respect of pension schemes

(a) *Preservation of rights under pension schemes – short-term employees*
    (i)   A 'short-term' member of a pension scheme is one who has had at least two years' pensionable service in an employment with a contracted-out pension scheme. Short-term employees must be provided with a preserved pension unless the accrued pension is transferred to another scheme.
    (ii)   The rules of the scheme must not contain any rules that will or could result in a disparity of treatment of a short-term pension scheme member as compared with the way in which a long-term member would be treated in the same circumstances.
    (iii)   Short-term members who have a preserved pension in a pension scheme must have their pensions increased to the same extent as those who remain in the scheme.

(b) *Choice of schemes*
The Act allows employees to opt for personal pension schemes rather than the employer's pension scheme and makes void any contractual provision which purports to make membership of the employer's occupational pension scheme mandatory.

(c) *Voluntary contributions*

Strict limitations are imposed on a scheme's ability to restrict a member's entitlement to make additional contributions to the scheme.

(d) *Disclosure of information*

The Secretary of State is empowered to make Regulations to require that certain categories of people are entitled to be given information about pension schemes. (Several sets of Regulations have been made under these provisions.)

The people who are entitled to this information are:

- members and, in the case of an occupational pension scheme, prospective members
- spouses of the above
- those to whom the scheme is applicable or prospectively applicable; and
- in the case of an occupational pension scheme, an independent trade union that is recognised to any degree for collective bargaining purposes.

The above categories of people can be required, by Regulations, to be kept informed of:

- the constitution of the scheme
- the scheme's administration and finances
- the rights and obligations that arise or may arise under the scheme
- any other matters which appear to the Secretary of State to be relevant either to:
  - occupational or personal pension schemes in general; or to
  - schemes of a description to which the scheme in question belongs.

The Regulations can specify when the required information is to be given as a matter of course and where it need be given only on application.

Where a person who is entitled to any such information is not given it then they must serve a default notice on the trustees. If they still do not get the information within a further 14 days then they can apply to the county court for an Order that the information be provided.

(e) *Pensions Ombudsman*

The Act establishes a Pensions Ombudsman who can deal with disagreements between a member of a pension scheme (or his dependants) and the trustees or managers of the scheme. The Ombudsman is empowered to deal with problems of all types, whether they are matters of fact, of law or of alleged maladministration. The Pensions Ombudsman's powers are amended by the Pensions Act 1995.

74 Personal Protective Equipment at Work Regulations 1992 (SI 1992 No. 2966)

This is one of the 'Six-pack' Regulations introduced in 1992 arising from European health and safety directives. The Regulations amend the Factories Act 1961.

(a) Personal protective equipment (PPE) is industrial body armour. Because it is cumbersome and uncomfortable for the wearer the Regulations, as a whole,

encourage PPE to be used only in the last resort where other forms of protection cannot be used or are inadequate. Where PPE is used a risk assessment must first be carried out to ensure that the PPE proposed is suitable and it is obviously important that all the PPE supplied to an employee is mutually compatible.
(b) Where PPE is provided it must be maintained in an efficient and clean state and in good repair. Proper accommodation must also be made available for its storage.
(c) The employee must be given training on the use and purpose of the PPE and on keeping it in a proper condition and must report any defect in, or loss of, the PPE to his employer. Both the employer and the employee are under a duty to ensure that the PPE is used properly.
(e) The Regulations contain several pages of guidance to help employers to select appropriate PPE for their particular needs.

74A   Police (Health and Safety) Act 1997

Amends Health and Safety at Work etc. Act 1974 and Employment Rights Act 1996.

Extends the general protection of employees under Part 1 Health and Safety at Work etc. Act 1974 to cover Police Officers. Police Officers are also given the right not to be dismissed for health and safety reasons and, as with other employees, any such dismissal is treated as being automatically unfair.

75   Police Act 1997

Amends Offices, Shops and Railway Premises Act 1963, Employers' Liability (Compulsory Insurance) Act 1969, Employers' Liability (Defective Equipment) Act 1969, Employment Agencies Act 1973, Sex Discrimination Act 1975, Race Relations Act 1976, Income and Corporation Taxes Act 1988, ERA.

The provisions of the Police Act 1997 that are relevant for employment purposes are a new system whereby Certificates of Criminal Records can be issued. It is intended that the Certificates under these provisions will be issued by a separate body set up specifically for this purpose. No date has been set for this legislation to take effect. (The legislation was passed by the last Conservative Government shortly before the 1997 General Election.)
(a) *Criminal Conviction Certificate*
  (i)   Under the new legislation anyone can apply to the Secretary of State for a Criminal Conviction Certificate provided that:
    • the application is made on a prescribed form and
    • the appropriate fee is paid.
  (ii) A Criminal Conviction Certificate gives details of any criminal convictions the person may have, other than any spent convictions (for 'Spent convictions' see *Rehabilitation of Offenders Act 1975*).
(b) *Criminal Record Certificate*
  (i)   Where a person is being considered for employment, or is seeking to join a profession which is exempted from the provisions of the

Rehabilitation of Offenders Act 1975 (ie one where questions regarding spent convictions – 'exempted questions' – must be answered fully and truthfully by the applicant), then a Criminal Record Certificate (CRC) can be obtained.

(ii) An application for a CRC must be:
- made in the prescribed form
- accompanied by the appropriate fee
- countersigned by a 'registered person'. (A person or body can be registered on application to the Secretary of State if the person or body is likely to ask exempted questions.) The registered person must also certify that the CRC is required for purposes of an exempt question.

(iii) A CRC will give details of:
- any convictions – whether or not spent; and
- any cautions.

(iv) A copy of the CRC is sent to the registered person who signed the application.

(c) *Enhanced Criminal Record Certificate*

(i) Where an applicant is applying for certain types of employment or licence (see (ii) below) an Enhanced Criminal Record Certificate (ECRC) can be sought.

(ii) The form and method of application is much the same as for a normal CRC (see above) but, for an ECRC to be issued, the 'exempted question' must be being asked
- in the course of considering the applicant for a position whether paid or unpaid which either:
  - involves regularly caring for, training, supervising or being in sole charge of persons aged under 18; or
  - is of a kind specified in Regulations made by the Secretary of State which involves regularly caring for, training, supervising or being in sole charge of persons aged 18 or over
- for a purpose relating to any of the following:
  - gaming licence application
  - lotteries and lotteries management licence application
  - registration as a child minder
  - placing children with foster parents.

(iii) An ECRC will give details of all relevant information relating to the applicant which is recorded in central records.

The Secretary of State must also ask all Chief Police Officers in any relevant force to provide any and all information which in that Officer's opinion:
- might be relevant to the employment or other application which has given rise to the exempt question being asked and which ought to be included in the certificate; and

- ought not to be included in the certificate in the interests of the prevention of crime but which can be disclosed to a registered person (in a separate document to the ECRC) without harming the interests of the prevention of crime.

  (iv) A copy of the ECRC and any accompanying document is sent to the registered person who signed the application.

(d) *Accuracy*

  (i) Where an applicant believes that a CCC, CRC or ECRC is inaccurate he can apply to the Secretary of State in writing for a new certificate. Where the Secretary of State is satisfied that the certificate is inaccurate a new certificate must be given.

  (ii) The Secretary of State may require that an applicant for a certificate under these provisions has fingerprints taken to establish that person's identity. Any Regulations made under this provision may make provision for the destruction of the fingerprints in certain specified circumstances.

(e) *Unlawful disclosure*

  (i) A member, officer or employee of a registered body may disclose information from a certificate only to:

- a fellow member, officer or employee of the registered body in the course of his duties
- a member, officer or employee of the body which asked the registered person to obtain the information for them.

Any breach of this is a criminal offence.

  (ii) There are further provisions which make it a criminal offence for a person or body on whose behalf the information has been obtained to further disclose such information or for a person to whom any such information is disclosed to divulge it to anyone else.

75A Protection from Harassment Act 1997

Creates both criminal and civil liability for harassment.

(a) *Harassment*

  i) A person must not pursue a course of conduct which he knows, or ought to know, amounts to harassment of another.

  ii) A person 'ought to know' that his conduct amounts to harassment if a reasonable person with the same information would consider that that course of conduct amounted to harassment.

  iii) A person is not guilty of harassment if in the particular circumstances the course of conduct was reasonable.

- A 'course of conduct' for these purposes must include conduct on two or more occasions; and
- 'conduct' includes speech.

Harassment may be dealt with both as a criminal matter, involving a penalty of up to six months' imprisonment, or as a civil matter. In relation to a civil action damages may be awarded for both anxiety caused by the harassment and any financial loss resulting from it. There is no reason, in principle, why an employer cannot be guilty as an accessory to harassment or, more probably in practice, vicariously liable for an employee's harassment.

Injunctions may also be granted to prevent harassment.

(b) *Putting another in fear of violence*

A person who on at least two occasions puts a person in fear that violence will be used against him is guilty of an offence.

Again, there is no reason why an employer cannot be guilty as an accessory to harassment or, more probably in practice, vicariously liable for an employee's conduct.

76 Provision of Work Equipment Regulations (SI 1992 No. 2932) (revoked and re-enacted in Provision of Work Equipment Regulations 1998 (SI 1998 No. 2306))

This was one of the 'Six-pack' Regulations introduced in 1992 arising from European health and safety directives. The Regulations amend Offices, Shops and Railway Premises Act 1963 and Factories Act 1961.

76A Provision of Work Equipment Regulations 1998 (SI 1998 No. 2306)

This was originally one of the 'Six-pack' Regulations introduced in 1992 arising from European health and safety directives. The Provision of Work Equipment Regulations (SI 1992 No. 2932) were revoked and re-enacted with amendments, by these Regulations, to give effect to Council Directive 95/63/EC.

The primary requirements imposed by these Regulations are beyond the scope of this work in that they concern the suitability of machinery and work equipment for the job and the environment in which they are used. They require work equipment to conform to European standards and to have appropriate controls. Such matters will generally be taken into account in the purchase and installation of the work equipment. There are, however, some aspects of these Regulations that may affect employees at a more day-to-day level.

(a) *Maintenance and repair*
   (i)   There is a duty to ensure that all work equipment is properly maintained and repaired.
   (ii)   A maintenance log needs to be kept for each machine.

(b) *Use, repair and modification of dangerous machinery*
   Where the use of a machine is likely to involve risks to health and safety
   (i)   only people who are properly trained may use the machine (adequate training for using such machinery is also required); and
   (ii)   such equipment must be repaired or modified only by those who are properly trained.

This means that employers need to make sure that machine operators who are not properly trained do not make their own informal modifications or try to repair such machines.

(c) *Health and safety information*

Any person who uses, or who supervises the use of, work equipment must have adequate health and safety information and where appropriate readily comprehensible written instructions about the use of the equipment. This must include instructions on:

(i)   the conditions in which, and methods by which, the equipment may be used

(ii)   any foreseeable abnormal situations – and action to be taken if such a situation occurs

(iii)   any conclusions drawn from experience in using the particular equipment.

(d) *Guarding equipment and employees*

(i)   There is a requirement properly to guard machinery and to exclude people from the danger areas surrounding the equipment.

(ii)   It is important to ensure that maintenance can be carried out safely – if at all possible with the machine switched off.

(iii)   There is a requirement to protect employees against anything coming off or out of any piece of work equipment and giving rise to injury; this includes protection against bits flying off, fire, discharge of any particle, dust or gas, etc.

(iv)   Employees must be protected against very high or low temperatures generated by parts of the machine.

(e) *Mobile work equipment*

i)   Mobile work equipment must not be used to carry an employee unless it is suitable for carrying people and it incorporates features to reduce to a minimum risks to their safety.

ii)   Where there is any risk of mobile work equipment rolling over this must be minimised and if there is a danger of the employee being crushed a suitable restraining system must be provided for the employee.

iii)   Self-propelling equipment must be used only by authorised people. There are also various specific requirements to do with the safe use of self-propelling equipment.

(f) *Inspection*

i)   Where the safety of the equipment depends on installation conditions the equipment must be inspected after installation or assembly at a new site or location, before being put into service.

ii)   Equipment exposed to deterioration which is likely to cause a dangerous situation must be inspected at suitable intervals or if an event occurs which is liable to jeopardise the safety of the equipment.

(g) *Working conditions*

(i)   The stability of the machine when in use must be ensured. This is particularly important in the case of portable machinery.

(ii)   The suitability and sufficiency of the lighting for the work that is carried out with the machine must also be ensured.

76B   Public Interest Disclosure Act 1998

Came into force on 2 July 1999. The Act takes effect by inserting a series of new sections into the Employment Rights Act 1996

(a) *Protected disclosure*

A protected disclosure is a 'qualifying disclosure' which is made to certain specified people or in certain specified circumstances. A contractual duty of confidentiality is void insofar as it purports to prevent a worker from making a protected disclosure.

(b) *Qualifying disclosure*

  i)   A qualifying disclosure is the disclosure of information by a worker which in the worker's reasonable belief shows that one or more of the following ('failures') has occurred, is happening or is likely to occur:
  - the commission of a criminal offence
  - a failure to comply with a legal obligation
  - the endangerment of anyone's health and safety
  - environmental damage; or
  - the deliberate concealment of information tending to show any of the above.

  ii) The failure can have occurred anywhere in the world.

  iii) The disclosure is not a qualifying disclosure if:
  - the person commits an offence in making it; or
  - it is disclosure by a lawyer who has come upon the information while advising a client.

(c) *To whom the disclosure may be made*

  i)   A disclosure will be protected only if made in good faith to one of the following:
  - the worker's employer or a person authorised to hear such disclosures under a policy or procedure dealing with such disclosures, where the employee reasonably believes that the failure relates solely or mainly to:
    - the conduct of someone other than his employer; or
    - a matter for which a person other than his employer has legal responsibility
    - the person whose conduct is in question or who is legally responsible for that conduct
  - the employee's legal adviser to obtain legal advice
  - if the employee is employed by a person who is, or by a body whose members are, appointed by a Minister of the Crown – to a Minister of the Crown
  - where the Secretary of State has prescribed someone to whom certain types of disclosure may be made and (then disclosure will be protected if) the employee reasonably believes:
    - that the matter is one in respect of which that person has been prescribed by the Secretary of State; and

- that the information disclosed and any allegations made are substantially true.

Under the Public Interest Disclosure (Prescribed Persons) Order 1999 a number of people are prescribed to receive information regarding various matters over which there is public control. These range from the Audit Commission – where matters of public business and value for money are concerned – to the Charity Commissioners – where administration of charitable funds is concerned.

ii) There is a series of disclosures which will be protected only if certain prerequisites are first met
  - prerequisites:
    - the worker makes the disclosure in good faith
    - he reasonably believes that the disclosure made and any allegations contained in it are substantially true
    - he does not make the disclosure for personal gain
    - in all the circumstances it is reasonable for him to make the disclosure (see below for further matters to be taken into account in respect of the reasonableness of the disclosure)
  - provided the above prerequisites are met the disclosure will be protected if made in one of the following sets of circumstances:
    - at the time of the disclosure the worker reasonably believes that he will be subjected to a detriment by his employer if he makes a disclosure either to his employer or to a person who has been prescribed for that purpose by the Secretary of State
    - there is no one prescribed for the worker to disclose the information to and the worker reasonably believes that the evidence will be concealed or withheld if he makes the disclosure to his employer
    - the worker has made disclosure of substantially the same information either to his employer or to a person who has been prescribed for that purpose by the Secretary of State
    - the relevant failure is of an exceptionally serious nature (what is of an exceptionally serious nature is not defined by the Act)
  - matters to be taken into account in deciding whether or not it was reasonable for the employee to make the disclosure:
    - in a situation falling under (d) above, the only matter to which regard is to be had is the person to whom the failure was disclosed
    - in all the cases under (a)–(c) regard must *also* be had to the following:
      - the seriousness of the failure
      - whether the failure is continuing or likely to re-occur in the future
      - where there was a previous disclosure to the employer or a prescribed person – what action the person to whom the disclosure was made might reasonably have been expected to take as a result of that previous disclosure

- where there was a previous disclosure to the employer – whether the employee followed any procedure laid down by the employer in making that disclosure

(d) *Definition of 'worker'*

As might be expected, the definition of a worker for these purposes is very wide indeed and includes not only those who work personally for the employer and agency and home workers, but also those who are on work experience with the employer.

(e) *Remedies*

  i)   The Act provides that a worker can make a claim if he is:
    - subjected to any detriment; or
    - dismissed
    for making any protected disclosure.
  ii) If the employee is dismissed for making a protected disclosure,
    - the dismissal is unfair;
    - any redundancy on that ground amounts to unfair dismissal
      - qualification for unfair dismissal rights
        - no qualifying service is required;
        - the upper age limit for claim does not apply; and
        - the exclusion of the right to claim for employees who are taking unofficial strike action does not apply
    - the Public Interest Disclosure (Compensation) Regulations 1999 provide that compensation is without limit
    - a worker who is not working under a contract of employment is entitled to the same compensation as an employee for these purposes
    - interim relief is also available.

77   Race Relations Act 1976

Repeals and replaces the Race Relations Acts 1965 and 1968.

Amended by Employment Act 1989, Further and Higher Education Act 1992, Education Act 1993 and Race Relations (Remedies) Act 1994, Armed Forces Act 1996, Police Act 1997, Employment Rights (Disputes Resolutions) Act 1998.

77.1   Grounds on which discrimination is unlawful

Makes discrimination unlawful on the grounds of colour, race, nationality or ethnic or national origin in employment and other fields. It is unlawful to discriminate against a person either directly or indirectly on these grounds.

77.2   Genuine occupational qualifications

Exceptions are made where race, etc., is a genuine occupational qualification for a particular job.

77.3   The Commission for Racial Equality

The Act established the Commission for Racial Equality (CRE) whose duties are:

(a) to work towards the elimination of racial discrimination; and
(b) to promote equality of opportunity and good relations between persons of different racial groups generally; and
(c) to monitor the working of the Act and to make recommendations to the Secretary of State to amend the Act if and when necessary.

The CRE is given wide powers of investigation and power to draw up codes of practice to eliminate discrimination in employment (see below). An employee or applicant for a job who has been discriminated against may be awarded compensation by an employment tribunal. The address of the CRE is:

Elliot House
10–12 Allington Street
London SW1E 5EH
Telephone: 020-7828 7022

CRE Code of Practice 1984

In April 1984 the CRE Code of Practice for the elimination of racial discrimination and the promotion of equality of opportunity in employment came into force. As with similar codes it is not legally binding but its provisions, and questions of whether or not an employer has complied with those provisions, are admissible in evidence before an employment tribunal. The Code's two most important recommendations on the responsibilities of employers concern:

1   the implementation of equal opportunities programmes; and
2   the monitoring of such programmes with the aid of analysis of the ethnic origins of the workforce and of job applicants.
        Specifically, the Code recommends that:
(a) employers should adopt, implement and monitor an equal opportunities policy
(b) the policy should be clearly communicated to all employees
(c) overall responsibility for the policy should be allocated to a member of senior management
(d) where appropriate, the policy should be discussed and agreed with trade unions or employee representatives
(e) training and guidance should be provided for supervisory staff and other relevant decision-makers to ensure they understand their position in law and under company policy
(f) employers should monitor the effects of selection decisions and of personnel practices/procedures to assess whether equal opportunity is being achieved. The information needed for effective monitoring may be obtained in a number of ways but, says the Code, will best be achieved by records showing the ethnic origins of existing employees and job applicants. (Abstracted from *IPM Digest*, No. 229, August 1984, pp9–10.)

78   Race Relations (Remedies) Act 1994

Amends the Race Relations Act 1976.

This Act was passed following the decision that the maximum limit on compensation fixed by the Sex Discrimination Act 1975, at that time £11,000, did not meet with the UK's obligation under European law to provide an adequate remedy in cases of sex discrimination. The upper limit of compensation in sex discrimination cases was removed by the Sex Discrimination and Equal Pay (Remedies) Regulations 1993 (SI 1993/2798) with effect from November 1993. The Race Relations (Remedies) Act 1994 abolished the upper limit on compensation for race discrimination with effect from 3 July 1994 by repealing s 56(2) of the RRA, thus bringing the remedies for sex and race discrimination back into line with each other.

78A   Redundancy Payments (Continuity of Employment in Local Government etc.) (Modification) Order 1999

Revokes the Redundancy Payments (Local Government) (Modification) Order 1983 and consolidates it and later amendments to it into a single Order with some further modification. The Order came into effect on 1 September 1999.

The Order provides that employment with certain named local government employers is to be treated as continuous with employment with other named local government employers. The effect is to treat a number of local government employers as if they were 'associated employers' for purposes of continuity of employment and in relation to offers of alternative work in a redundancy situation.

79   Rehabilitation of Offenders Act 1974

Amended by Armed Forces Act 1996

Provides that a convicted offender, other than one given a sentence of more than 30 months' imprisonment, may become rehabilitated if he commits no further serious offences during the rehabilitation period. The rehabilitation periods vary with the sentences imposed and the age of the offender is also taken into account. Where a conviction has expired, under the terms of the Act it is unlawful for the offender to be refused employment or to be dismissed from employment on the grounds of that conviction. Certain professions and occupations are excluded from the provisions of the Act; these include the legal profession, accountants and teachers.

80   Reserve Forces Act 1980

Amended by Reserve Forces (Safeguard of Employment) Act 1985 and greatly amended and replaced by the Reserve Forces Act 1996.

Amends Trade Union and Labour Relations Act 1974, Employment Protection (Consolidation) Act 1978.

The provision for reserve forces and Territorial Army to be called up are now contained in Part VI Reserve Forces Act 1996. They were previously made under

LIVERPOOL JOHN MOORES UNIVERSITY
LEARNING SERVICES

s 10 of the 1980 Act. Orders authorising the calling out of reserve forces/TA are made by the Queen, under the hand of the Secretary of State, under s 10 of the Act.

In the Gulf War such an order was made to protect the employment of reservists who volunteered for service with the forces as well as those who were called up (see also *Reserve Forces (Safeguard of Employment) Act 1985* below).

81 Reserve Forces Act 1996

Amends Reserve Forces (Safeguard of Employment) Act 1985.

Repeals and replaces much of the Reserve Forces Act 1980 and the whole of the Reserve Forces Act 1982.

81.1 Definition

Reserve Forces are: the Royal Fleet Reserve, Royal Naval Reserve, Royal Marine Reserve, Army Reserve, Territorial Army, Air Force Reserve and the Royal Auxiliary Air Force.

81.2 Calling up reserve forces

(a) The statutory provisions allowing for reserve forces to be called up are now contained in Part VI Reserve Forces Act 1996.

(b) Reserve forces may be called up
   - where the nation appears to be in imminent danger
   - where a great emergency has arisen or there is an actual or apprehended attack on the UK
   - where warlike operations are in preparation or progress
   - where the Secretary of State considers it desirable to use armed forces for:
      - the protection of life or property outside the United Kingdom; or
      - in operations anywhere in the world to save lives or property in time of disaster or apprehended disaster.

(c) In cases where an Order calling out reserve forces is made, the employment of those who are called up is protected under the Reserve Forces (Safeguard of Employment) Act 1985. In the Gulf War an order was made calling up reservists who had volunteered for service with the forces as well as those who were actually called up. This had the effect of ensuring that the employment of volunteers was protected under Reserve Forces (Safeguard of Employment) Act 1985.

81.3 Special agreements/Employee agreements

(a) *Special agreements*
   An employee who is employed to work for more than 14 hours per week may, with the consent of his employer, enter into an agreement that will make him liable:
   - to be called out for permanent service anywhere in the world; and
   - to fulfil any training obligations specified in the agreement for a period of up to nine months.

(b) *Employee agreements*
   (i) Employee agreements are agreements primarily between the employer and Secretary of State for employees to enter into agreements to become special members of the reserve forces.
   (ii) An employee can enter into an agreement to become a special member of the reserve forces in such circumstances with his employer's consent.
(c) A person who is called up under either of these schemes can seek a deferral or exemption from call-up.
(d) Employees who are called up under these schemes have their employment protected under the Reserve Forces (Safeguard of Employment) Act 1985.

81.4   Former members of the forces

(a) Former members of the regular forces are liable to be recalled unless they are 55 or over, or if they were discharged or transferred to the reserve forces 18 or more years previously. (Former members of the Royal Navy or Royal Marines remain liable to be recalled for only six years after discharge or transfer to the Reserves.)
(b) Employees who are recalled under these provisions have their employment protected under the Reserve Forces (Safeguard of Employment) Act 1985.

82   Reserve Forces (Safeguard of Employment) Act 1985

Amends Reserve Forces Act 1980, Employment Protection (Consolidation) Act 1978, Tribunals and Enquiries Act 1971.
   Repeals National Service Act 1948, Reinstatement in Civil Employment Act 1950.
   Amended by Reserve Forces Act 1996.
(a) *When is protection given?*
   The Act provides safeguards, in relation to employment, for: reservists and those who have entered into special or employee agreements who are called up into full-time service in the forces and those who are recalled to full-time service in the forces.
   (NB Those who volunteer for service without being called up are generally outside this statutory protection, but in the Gulf War an Order was made calling up volunteers so that their employment would be protected – see *Reserve Forces Act 1996* above.)
(b) *The rights provided for by the Act*
   (i) Right to return
       The Act provides for an employee who was employed within four weeks before being called up to be offered a job by his last employer, at the first reasonable opportunity after his release from full-time service, and to be kept in that job for no less than the minimum statutory period.
   (ii) Minimum statutory period
       The minimum statutory period for which the employee must be employed after returning from the forces depends on the employee's length of service before being called up.

If the employee had less than 13 or more than 26 or 52 weeks' employment before call-up he will be entitled to be kept on for at least 13, 26 or 52 weeks respectively, following his reinstatement. The only restriction on this right is that it must be reasonable and practicable for the employer to keep the employee on (or to keep him on the terms and conditions on which he was reinstated) throughout that period.

(iii)   Right to return to what?

The employee's right is primarily a right to be offered employment in the occupation in which he was engaged before his full-time service with the forces began, on terms and conditions no less favourable than those that would have applied had he not been away. If it is not reasonable and practicable for the employee to be taken back into his former occupation on those terms and conditions, then he is entitled to be offered a job in the most favourable occupation and on the most favourable terms and conditions that are reasonable and practicable in his case.

(iv)   Right to return when?

The employee must be offered employment to begin at the first opportunity (if any) at which it is reasonable and practicable for it to begin after the date that he has notified to the employer as the date on which he will be available for work (see (c) below).

The right to be offered a job is also limited to the first six months after the ex-employee's service with the forces ends. After this the former employer has no duty to take the employee back (unless he is required to take the employee back following any order to that effect made by a Reinstatement Committee).

(v)   Effect of refusing employer's offer

Once the employer has offered the employee a job, his obligation to take the employee back is *prima facie* discharged. However, it will not be discharged if the applicant believes that he has reasonable cause for not taking the job that is offered and he, or someone acting on his behalf, notifies the employer in writing of his reasons for not taking the job 'as soon as may be' after the job is offered.

(c)   *Enforcement of these statutory rights*

Either the applicant or someone acting on the applicant's behalf must apply in writing to the applicant's former employer asking that the applicant be taken back into employment. The application must be made within the first two weeks after the applicant's release from full-time service with the forces. If the applicant is sick, or if because of some other reasonable cause the applicant cannot apply within the prescribed time, the application will still be valid provided it is made as soon as it reasonably can be.

The applicant must also provide his former employer with a date when he will be available to take up work if it is offered. That date must be within 21 days of the latest date on which the application can be validly made (this is, again, extended where the applicant is sick or where it is otherwise reasonable for him not to comply).

An application to be taken back into employment ceases to have effect 13 weeks after it was made, unless it has been renewed during the 13-week period. It is also preserved during any period while there are any proceedings pending regarding the application.

An applicant can apply to a Reinstatement Committee if he considers that any of his rights under the Act (including his right to be taken back and to be kept on for the minimum statutory period) are being or have been denied to him.

(d) *Statutory presumptions as to whether or not it is reasonable and practicable to take an employee back*

The Act provides that the fact that taking the applicant back will involve dismissing someone else does not, of itself, make taking the applicant back either unreasonable or impracticable. The only exception to this is where taking the employee back would involve dismissing another employee who had been employed for longer than the applicant by the date when the applicant left employment to join the forces. Where both the applicant and the other employee were called up then the comparison is between the length of service given by each before the first of them left to join the forces.

(e) *Continuity of employment*

Employees who are entitled to apply to be employed by their former employer, and who are taken back within six months of the termination of their full-time service with the forces, have their employment before they were called up treated as continuous with their employment after their return to work. The actual period of absence does not itself count as a period of continuous employment.

83   Safety Representatives and Safety Committees Regulations 1977 (SI 1977 No. 500)

The Regulations were amended by the Management of Health and Safety at Work Regulations 1992 (SI 1992 No. 2051) and by Health and Safety (Consultation with Employees) Regulations 1996 (SI 1996 No. 1513).

These Regulations were made under the Health and Safety at Work etc. Act 1974 and provide for consultation where trade unions are recognised. Where trade unions are not recognised employers are required to consult either the employees themselves or representatives of employee safety, under the Health and Safety (Consultation with Employees) Regulations 1996 (SI 1996 No. 1513) (*qv*).

(a) *Appointment of safety representatives*

   (i)   Where an independent trade union is recognised by an employer then the union can appoint safety representatives. The union must inform the employer in writing who they have appointed.

   (ii) Employees appointed as safety representatives should normally have had two years in that employment or in similar employment so that they have experience of the type of workplace.

(b) *Functions of safety representatives*
  (i)   The employer must consult safety representatives with a view to:
  - establishing and maintaining arrangements for effective co-operation between the employer and his employees; to ensure the health and safety at work of employees; and
  - checking the effectiveness of those arrangements
    - on the introduction of:
      - any measures that may substantially affect employees' health and safety; and
      - new technology
  - arrangements for:
    - appointing people to be responsible for statutory health and safety duties
    - nominating people to deal with serious and imminent dangers at work and danger areas
  - health and safety information which he is required by statute to provide
  - planning of health and safety training he is required by statute to provide.
  (ii)   To carry out inspections of the workplace
  - once every three months after giving written notice to the employer; or
  - more often:
    - with the employer's consent
    - where there has been a substantial change in the conditions of work, such as the introduction of new machinery, since the last inspection
    - where relevant advice from the Health and Safety Executive (HSE) has been given since the last inspection
    - where there has been a notifiable accident or dangerous occurrence or where a notifiable disease has been contracted. In such cases safety representatives may inspect the area affected and any other areas that it is necessary to inspect to determine the cause.

The employer may accompany the safety representative on any such inspection.
  (iii) To investigate
  - potential hazards at the workplace
  - dangerous occurrences at the workplace
  - causes of accidents at the workplace
  - complaints by employees relating to their health and safety at work.
  (iv)   To make representations to the employer
  - arising out of the above investigations; and
  - on general matters affecting the health, safety and welfare of the employees at the workplace.
  (v)   To represent employees in consultations with the Health and Safety inspectorate.
  (vi)   To attend Safety Committee meetings as a safety representative.

(c) *Requirement to provide information and documentation*
  (i)   The employer must provide information for safety representatives so that they have all the relevant information that the employer has available which will allow them to carry out their duties. Certain types of confidential information are excluded from this requirement.
  (ii) The employer must allow safety representatives to inspect and take copies of all health and safety documentation which the employer is obliged by statute to keep – other than documentation relating to an identifiable individual.
(d) *Facilities*
  (i)   Safety representatives are entitled to paid time off:
    • to carry out their duties as safety representatives; and
    • to undergo training.
  (ii) If a safety representative is refused paid time off he can complain to an employment tribunal within three months of the time off being refused (or where that is not reasonably practicable within such further time as is reasonably practicable).
  (iii) The employer must provide safety representatives with such facilities and assistance as they may reasonably require to carry out their duties.
(e) *Safety committees*
  (i)   An employer must establish a safety committee where two or more safety representatives request him to do so in writing.
  (ii) Where safety representatives request the establishment of a safety committee the employer must:
    • consult with those representatives and trade union representatives in the areas that will be covered by the safety committee
    • post a notice, giving the composition of the safety committee, where all relevant employees will be able to see it; and
    • establish the safety committee within three months of the request being made.

84   Sex Discrimination Act 1975

Amended by Employment Act 1989, Further and Higher Education Act 1992 and Education Act 1993 and Sex Discrimination and Equal Pay (Remedies) Regulations 1993 (SI 1993/2798), Pensions Act 1995, Armed Forces Act 1996, Police Act 1997, Employment Rights (Disputes Resolutions) Act 1998, Sex Discrimination (Gender Reassignment) Regulations 1999.

Makes discrimination on grounds of sex or marital status unlawful. Its provisions are similar in extent and effect to those of the Race Relations Act 1976. The main differences are:
(a) the Sex Discrimination Act (SDA) does not cover discrimination in pay – this is dealt with by the Equal Pay Act 1970 as amended.
(b) the SDA makes special provision to deal with discrimination in matters relating to death or retirement (amended by SDA 1986, Employment Act

1989 and prospectively by the Pensions Act 1995 – see commentary under *Sex Discrimination Act 1986*). The SDA excludes special, more beneficial, provisions relating to pregnancy from being treated as discrimination.

(c) the Equal Opportunities Commission (EOC) is established by the Act and has an equivalent function to the Commission for Racial Equality (CRE) in matters related to sex discrimination, including the power to draw up codes of practice (see below). The EOC also has jurisdiction to monitor and review the working of the Equal Pay Act 1970.

85 Sex Discrimination Act 1986

Amended by Employment Act 1989 and ERA its provisions are also amended by the Pensions Act 1995.

Amends Sex Discrimination Act 1975, Employment Protection (Consolidation) Act 1978, Equal Pay Act 1970, Employment Protection Act 1975, Hours of Work Convention Act 1936, Factories Act 1961, Health and Safety at Work etc. Act 1974.

85.1 Employment in private households

The Act removes the right to discriminate, on grounds of sex, where employment is for a private household, except in a case where the amount of intimate contact with a person living in the home or the knowledge of intimate details of a person's life which the employee might come upon means that the householder might reasonably object to having a man/woman do that work.

85.2 Death and retirement

The exclusion of matters related to 'death or retirement' from the sex discrimination legislation under the 1975 Act is largely removed. Whereas in the normal case it is unlawful for an employer to discriminate by dismissing an employee or subjecting her to any other detriment, in cases where the discrimination is concerned with retirement it is unlawful to discriminate by 'dismissing or subjecting [the individual] to any detriment which results in her dismissal or consists in or involves her demotion'. This still allows some scope for discrimination in relation to pension matters. There is an equivalent provision inserted into the Equal Pay Act 1970. The provisions regarding discrimination in relation to pensions are, however, prospectively modified by the Pensions Act 1995 to allow for unequal treatment of men and women in a pension scheme where that treatment would not offend against the 'equal treatment' requirements under the Pension Act 1995.

85.3 Normal retirement age

The 1986 Act amended the exclusion, from claiming unfair dismissal, for those over normal retirement age or statutory pension age so that an employee's claim is excluded only if he has reached either:

(a) 'normal retirement age' for a person holding that position in the organisation (provided that that retirement age is the same for both men and women); or

(b) in any other case, 65.

This provision is now contained in s 109 ERA.

85.4   Terms in collective agreements

The Act invalidates any terms in collective agreements, in an employer's rule and in the rules of qualifying bodies, which are unlawfully discriminatory or which give rise to unlawful discrimination.

85.5   Women's hours of work

The erstwhile restrictions on women's hours of work, under various statutes, are removed.

The address of the EOC is:

Overseas House
Quay Street
Manchester M3 3HN
Tel. 0161-833 9244

86   Sex Discrimination and Equal Pay (Remedies) Regulations 1993 (SI 1993/2798)

Amends the Sex Discrimination Act 1975.

These regulations were passed following the decision that the maximum limit on compensation fixed by the Sex Discrimination Act 1975, at that time £11,000, did not meet with the UK's obligation under European law to provide an adequate remedy in cases of sex discrimination. These regulations remove the upper limit of compensation in sex discrimination cases by repealing s 65(2) Sex Discrimination Act 1975. They came into operation with effect from 22 November 1993.

EOC Code of Practice 1985

The EOC launched its Code of Practice for the elimination of discrimination on grounds of sex or marital status in employment on 30 April 1985. The Code is divided into two main parts. The first deals with the role of good employment practices in eliminating sex and marriage discrimination and the second with the role of good employment practices in promoting equality of opportunity. The Code does not carry the force of law but both parts will be taken into account by employment tribunals in proceedings under the Sex Discrimination Acts. As with the CRE Code of Practice that has been in force since April 1984, one of the key recommendations is the formulation and implementation of an equal opportunities policy which, says the EOC, 'will ensure the effective use of human resources in the best interests of both the organisation and its employees'. In summary, the Code's main suggestions for successfully implementing an equal opportunities policy are:

1.   The policy must be seen to have the active support of top management.

2. The policy should be clearly stated and, where appropriate, should be included in a collective agreement.
3. Overall responsibility for implementing the policy should rest with senior management.
4. The policy should be made known to all employees and, where reasonably practicable, to all job applicants.
5. Trade unions have an important part to play in implementing genuine equality of opportunity and will obviously be involved in the review of established procedures to ensure they are consistent with the law.
6. The policy should be monitored regularly to ensure that it is working in practice.
7. In a small firm it may be quite adequate to assess the distribution and payment of employees from personal knowledge.
8. In a large, complex organisation a more formal analysis will be necessary, for example, by sex, grade and payment in each unit. This may need to be introduced by stages as resources permit.
9. Sensible monitoring will show, for example, whether members of one sex:
    (a) do not apply for employment or promotion, or whether fewer apply than might be expected
    (b) are not recruited, promoted or selected for training development or are appointed/selected in a significantly lower proportion than their rate of application
    (c) are concentrated in certain jobs, sections or departments.

Other aspects covered by the Code include job advertising, selection methods – with particular reference to the avoidance of certain discriminatory questions at interviews – promotion, transfer and training, terms of employment, grievance and disciplinary procedures and victimisation. (Abstracted from the *IPM Digest*, No. 238, May 1985, pp1–2.)

86A   Sex Discrimination (Gender Reassignment) Regulations 1999

Amend the Sex Discrimination Act 1975 to give effect to the ECJ's judgement in *P v S and Cornwall County Council* [1996] IRLR 347, where it was held that discrimination on grounds of gender reassignment is unlawful under Council Directive 76/207/EC.

(a) Gender reassignment is defined as 'a process which is undertaken under medical supervision for the purpose of reassigning a person's sex by changing physiological or other characteristics of sex and includes any part of such a process'.
(b) A person discriminates unlawfully if he treats a person who intends to undergo, is undergoing or has undergone gender reassignment less favourably on those grounds than he treats or would treat others in relation to employment or vocational training.
(c) Exceptions:

i) where sex is a genuine occupational qualification (within the existing terms of the Sex Discrimination Act 1975); and the employer can show that the treatment is reasonable in view of:
  - the particular genuine occupational qualification; and
  - any other relevant circumstances.

ii) supplementary genuine occupational qualifications are also added for cases of gender reassignment:
  - the job holder is likely to be called upon to perform intimate physical searches pursuant to statutory powers
  - the job holder is working or living in a private home and objection might reasonably be taken to allowing a person who is or who has undergone gender reassignment the degree of physical or social contact with a person living in the home or the knowledge of intimate details of his life.
  - where the person intends to or is undergoing gender reassignment there are two further supplementary genuine occupational qualifications:
    - where the person undertaking the job has to live on the premises and reasonable objection could be taken for purposes of decency or privacy to sharing accommodation while undergoing gender reassignment and it is not reasonable to expect the employer to equip the premises with suitable accommodation or to make alternative arrangements
    - where the job holder provides vulnerable individuals with services promoting their welfare or similar services and in the employer's reasonable view those services cannot be effectively provided by a person while undergoing gender reassignment.

(d) A specific provision is put in to deal with absence from work due to gender reassignment. A person is deemed to be treated less favourably if, in relation to any arrangements for absence due to gender reassignment:
  - he is treated less favourably than he would be if the absence was due to sickness or injury; or
  - he is treated less favourably than he would be if the absence was due to some other cause and, having regard to the circumstances of the case, it is reasonable for him to be treated no less favourably.

(e) Discrimination in relation to pay on grounds of gender reassignment is dealt with under the terms of the Sex Discrimination Act 1975, as amended, rather than under the Equal Pay Act 1970.

87   Sex Disqualification (Removal) Act 1919

Provides that no person shall by reason of sex or marriage be excluded from any public function, any judicial or civil office or post 'or from entering or assuming or carrying on any civil profession or vocation, or for the admission of any incorporated society (whether incorporated by Royal Charter or otherwise) . . .'.

88 Shops Acts 1950–1965

Amended by Employment Act 1989 and Deregulation and Contracting Out Act 1994, the relevant provisions of the latter were consolidated into the ERA.

Designed to ensure that shop assistants do not have to work excessive hours and that they are allowed adequate rest periods. (See also *Offices, Shops and Railway Premises Act 1963.*) Certain restrictions on shop workers' working on Sundays were removed by the Deregulation and Contracting Out Act 1994, the relevant provisions of which have been consolidated into the Employment Rights Act 1996.

89 Social Security Acts 1975, (No. 2) 1980, 1985, 1986, 1988 and 1990 and the Social Security Pensions Act 1975 and the Social Security and Housing Benefits Act 1982 (repealed/consolidated)

These Acts have been largely repealed and consolidated into the Social Security (Contributions and Benefits) Act 1992 and the Pension Schemes Act 1993.

90 Social Security Act 1989

Amended by Employment Act 1990, Social Security Act 1990, Pension Schemes Act 1993 and Pensions Act 1995.

Amends Social Security Acts 1986 and 1988.

Section 23 and Schedule 5 of the Act were enacted to give effect to EC Directive 86/378/EEC on equal treatment for men and women in relation to occupational social security schemes. The main area in which these provisions were intended to operate was in relation to pension schemes. But this changed dramatically following the ECJ's judgment in *Barber* v *Guardian Royal Exchange Assurance Group* [1990] IRLR 240 and a number of later cases, which further explained the European equal treatment requirements in relation to pension schemes. Equal treatment under occupational pension schemes from 17 May 1990, the date of the ECJ's judgment in Barber, had to be treated as a matter of equal pay which meant that it had to be dealt with rather more stringently than was envisaged by the 1989 provisions. The provisions of this Act, insofar as they relate to pension schemes, were, therefore, overtaken by the Pensions Act 1995. The only areas in which the 1989 provisions have been brought into effect are unfair maternity and family leave provisions. It should be borne in mind that these are social security measures and, as such, apply to social security as well as employment benefits.

(a) *Entitlement to equal treatment*
- A woman during a period of paid maternity leave and a person during a period of paid family leave (ie a period throughout which the employee is on leave for family reasons) are entitled not to be treated less favourably in relation to any employment-related benefit schemes than they would be if they were at work. This means that:
  - any continuing rights they may have under the scheme must be equivalent to those that would have applied if they had not been on leave; and

- where their overall entitlement under a scheme takes into account a period of maternity or family leave, they must again be in an equivalent position to that which would have applied if they had not been on leave.
- Schemes are, however, specifically permitted to provide more favourable treatment for women who are on maternity leave.
- Where the employee pays into the scheme then the amount that she is required to pay during her maternity leave or family leave must be based on the amount that she is actually being paid during that period.
- Where these requirements are not complied with, and less favourable treatment is given to a woman on maternity leave or to a person on family leave, then she can claim entitlement to the more beneficial treatment afforded to other equivalent members of the scheme:
  - in the case of a woman on maternity leave her treatment must be no less favourable than other women members of the scheme
  - in the case of those on family leave they are to be treated no less favourably than they would be if they were working normally but being paid only what they are actually paid during their family leave.

(b) *Schemes to which the requirements apply*
  - These requirements apply to any of the following types of scheme which are employment-related and which provide different levels of benefit dependent on service. They apply even if the scheme is a discretionary one, provided only that the benefits under the scheme are payable in money or in money's worth. Relevant schemes are those providing benefit in respect of:
    - termination of service
    - retirement, old age or death
    - time off because of sickness or invalidity
    - accidents, injuries or diseases connected with employment
    - unemployment; or
    - expenses incurred in connection with children or other dependants;
    and in the case of an employee, include any such benefits which are payable as a result of that person's employment.
  - The following types of scheme are, however, excluded from these provisions:
    - any personal scheme for employees to which the employer does not contribute
    - any insurance scheme which is for the benefit of employees and to which the employer is not a party.

91   Social Security Administration Act (SSAA) 1992

Amended by Statutory Sick Pay Act 1994 and Jobseekers Act 1995.

Together with the Social Security Contributions and Benefits Act (SSCBA) 1992 consolidates most social security law. The SSCBA deals with the substantive law and the SSAA deals with the administrative parts.

91.1 Investigation, inspection and disclosure of documents

These provisions were originally in the Social Security Act 1986. The Act provides for the appointment of inspectors who are given certain powers.

(a) *Power to enter premises*

An inspector has power under this provision to enter premises where he has reasonable grounds for supposing:

(i)   that there are people employed; or

(ii)   that any type of employment agency or 'employment business' is being carried on; or

(iii)   that an occupational health scheme is being run or administered from those premises.

Private dwellings that are not used for business purposes by the occupier (or with his permission) are excluded from this provision.

If requested to do so the inspector must produce a certificate of his appointment when seeking to enter any premises.

(b) *Extent of powers*

An inspector's powers extend to:

(i)   entering premises liable to inspection at all reasonable times

(ii)   making such examination and enquiry as may be necessary for estimating whether the provisions of the various benefits acts are being complied with

(iii)   making such examination and enquiry as may be necessary for investigating any circumstances giving rise to any industrial injuries benefit claim

(iv)   examining anyone whom he reasonably believes might be liable to pay Social Security contributions of any sort

(v)   requiring the production of information in accordance with (c) below.

(c) *Disclosure of information to an inspector*

During an inspection those asked are required to provide the inspector with all the information and documentation he may reasonably require, for purposes either of ascertaining:

(i)   whether or not any Social Security contributions are payable in respect of any person and, if they are, whether or not those contributions have been duly paid; or

(ii)   whether benefit under any of the benefits acts is or was payable in respect of any person. (This is a potentially far-reaching provision which provides a facility for ensuring that the employees are not also receiving Jobseekers' Allowance or other undeclared social security benefits.)

In practice, requests for disclosure of information are usually made by post.

91.2 Employer's and employee's notification requirements in respect of SSP and SMP

(a) This Act now contains the requirements for employees to provide their employers with proper medical information of

• any time off for sickness; and

- the expected date of confinement in maternity cases.
(b) The Act also requires employers, if requested to do so by an employee, to provide a statement specifying any days within a period in the case of SSP (or of any weeks within a period, in the case of SMP):
    (i) in which he considers he is liable to pay the employee SSP or SMP
    (ii) the reason why he does not consider he is liable to pay the employee SSP or SMP for the other days/weeks in that period; and
    (iii) the amount of SSP/SMP that the employer considers himself liable to pay in respect of each of the days or weeks in question.

92　Social Security (Consequential Amendments) Act 1992

This Act was used to repeal the various provisions that needed to be repealed as a consequence of the two social security consolidating statutes: the Social Security Contributions and Benefits Act 1992 and the Social Security Administration Act 1992.

93　Social Security Contributions and Benefits Act 1992 (SSCBA)

Amended by Statutory Sick Pay Act 1994, Social Security (Incapacity for Work) Act 1994 and Jobseekers Act 1995.

Together with the Social Security Administration Act 1992, this Act consolidated a great deal of social security law, the SSCBA dealing with the substantive law and the SSAA dealing with the administrative parts. Most important for employment purposes is the consolidation of the law relating to SSP and SMP.

93.1　Statutory Sick Pay (SSP)

(a) *The benefit*
    (i) Statutory Sick Pay (SSP) is payable by the employer to an employee for any day of incapacity for work in respect of which the employee meets the statutory qualifications.
    (ii) SSP is a flat-rate benefit. An employee's maximum entitlement in any one Period of Entitlement (see (c) (iii) below) is 28 times the weekly SSP rate.
    (iii) SSP is subject to income tax and National Insurance.
    (iv) Daily rate for payment where the employee is entitled for part weeks is: SSP weekly rate × number of Q days for which payment is due ÷ Agreed number of Q days per week (see 93.1(c)(iv) for the definition of 'Q day')
    (v) Any contractual sick pay goes towards discharging the employer's liability to pay SSP and vice versa.
    (vi) Employers were originally able to recoup the costs of SSP. This facility has now been removed except in very restricted cases – for the current position see Statutory Sick Pay Act 1994.

(vii) Any agreement between an employer and employee for the employer not to pay the employee the SSP to which he is entitled is void. This does not, however, prevent an employer from making deductions from SSP to the same extent as could be made from the employee's normal pay. So where there is a pre-existing arrangement, for example where deductions are being made in respect of the repayment of a loan, those deductions can continue to be made from any SSP that would otherwise be payable.

(b) *Who is covered?*

   (i) All employees over 16 and who are employed in Great Britain and who pay Class 1 National Insurance contributions (including married women and widows who pay at a lower rate).

   (ii) Part-timers, provided their earnings are above the Lower Earnings Limit for NI contributions.

   (iii) Those with two jobs can claim from both employers.

(c) *Qualification for entitlement*

There are five qualifications for entitlement.

   (i) The day must be a day of incapacity for work.

- A 'day of incapacity for work' means a day when the employee is, because of a disease or physical or mental disablement, incapable of doing work which he could reasonably be expected to do under his contract of employment.
- Under the Statutory Sick Pay (General) Regulations 1982 (SI 1982 No. 894) an employee who is sick at the beginning of the day or during the working day is deemed to be incapable of work for the whole day if he does no work during that day.

   (ii) The day in question must form part of the Period of Incapacity for Work (PIW).

- A PIW is a period of four or more consecutive days during which the employee is incapable of work due to sickness.
- For purposes of a PIW all days of incapacity for work count – regardless of whether or not the employee would normally be working on that day. This also applies to days of incapacity for work which occur before the contract begins and after it ends.
- Any two PIWs that are separated by not more than eight weeks form a single PIW. This means that the employee will not have to be without SSP during the 'waiting days' which would otherwise apply to the later, linked, PIW (for 'waiting days', see below).

   (iii) The day must be part of the Period of Entitlement (PE).

- A PE begins at the beginning of the PIW and ends when:
  - the employee's PIW ends
  - the employee's entitlement to SSP from that employer is exhausted
  - his employment has ended; or
  - a pregnant employee reaches the 'disqualifying period' (ie 18 weeks

beginning with the 11th week before the expected week of confinement).

- A PE does not arise where, at the date when a PE would otherwise begin:
  - the employee is over the age of 65 (the age was increased from 60 for women by the Statutory Sick Pay Act 1994)
  - the employee is under a fixed-term contract of three months or less (unless the employee has actually been employed for more than three months – either under the contract in question, or under one or more contracts each separated by eight weeks or less)
  - the employee is earning less than the lower earnings limit for NI contributions
  - during the 57 days prior to the day in question the employee had at least one day where he was entitled to:
    - incapacity benefit
    - maternity allowance; or
    - severe disablement allowance
  - the employee has done no work under his contract of employment (NB Where the employee was employed by the same employer less than eight weeks before the start date of the contract in question, the two contracts are treated as one.)
  - on the day in question there is a trade dispute at the employee's place of work unless the employee can show that he had no interest in that dispute at any time either on or before the day in question
  - the employee is or has been pregnant and the day falls within the disqualifying period unless her pregnancy ended (otherwise than by confinement) before the disqualifying period began.

    Where an employee in an excluded category is off sick for four or more consecutive days the employer must complete and send to the employee an exclusion form within 11 days of the employee's first day off sick.

(iv) The day must be a qualifying day (Q day).
- Q days are those days which, subject to Regulations, the employer and the employee have agreed as being either:
  - the days on which the employee would normally be required to work under his contract; or
  - days which are chosen to reflect the employee's normal working pattern.
- The agreement as to Q days is left largely to the employer and employee but:
  - there must be at least one Q day per week
  - the Q days can vary from week to week
  - Q days must be specified

- if no Q days are agreed then Q days will normally be those days on which the employee would be required to work.

  Alternatively, if these cannot be agreed, Q days will be those days which are not specifically agreed to be rest days.

  NB A restriction on the ability of employers and employees to agree Q days was introduced by the Statutory Sick (General) Amendment Regulations 1985 (SI 1985 No. 126). This prevents 'maximising' SSP by setting Q days as being those days when the employee is off sick.

- The employee is not entitled to be paid for the first three Q days in any PIW – these are known as 'waiting days'.

(v)   The absence is duly notified and certified.

- The notification requirements are left to the employer but:
  - he cannot require notification before the first Q day
  - he cannot require notification by a specific time of day (ie notification can be insisted on only by the end of the first Q day)
  - the employer must specify whether notification should be oral or written or both (if written and posted it is the day of posting which is the day of notification)
  - the employer cannot demand notification by the employee in person
  - the employer cannot demand notification in the form of medical evidence of sickness or on a printed form
  - the employer cannot demand notification more than once every seven days during a PE.
- Where notification is late then the employer has discretion to treat the days before notification is given as not being Q days (ie he can withhold SSP and treat the first three Q days after notification as waiting days).
- The Act requires that the employer must obtain suitable evidence of incapacity. This will usually take the form of medical certificates. (See also *Social Security (Medical Evidence, Claims and Payments) Amendment Regulations 1982–95* below.)

93.2   Statutory Maternity Pay (SMP)

The Statutory Maternity Pay provisions came into effect for women whose expected date of confinement was after 21 June 1987. They were brought in by the Social Security Act 1986. The following outline of the Statutory Maternity Pay scheme deals with the provisions of both the Act and various Regulations made under the Act.

(a)   *Qualifications for SMP*

To qualify for entitlement to SMP a woman must (subject to very limited exceptions that are not dealt with here) fulfil all of the following requirements:

(i)   She must be over the age of 16.

(ii)   She must be employed under a contract of employment (ie be an employee rather than self-employed).

(iii) She must have completed not less than 26 weeks' continuous service by some time during the 15th week before the Expected Week of Confinement (EWC).

It is noteworthy that the woman need only work during the 15th week before the EWC – she need not work out the whole of that week. (A 'week' for SMP purposes starts from midnight on Saturday night.)

(iv) She must have had normal weekly earnings that were not lower than the Lower Earnings Limit for NI contributions for the eight weeks of employment ending with the 15th week before the EWC (NB *Normal weekly earnings* are the employee's average earnings over this eight-week period. This means that she would not necessarily have to earn more than the Lower Earnings Limit in each of these weeks.)

(v) She must have given her employer notice at least 21 days in advance of her absence, stating that she is going to be absent from work wholly or partly because of pregnancy or confinement. This notice must be given in writing if the employer so requests. (NB If the woman also intends to return to work – and has a statutory right to return – after extended maternity leave then she will have to give written notice both of the fact that she is leaving to go on maternity leave and that she intends to return to work. A woman who is entitled only to the statutory minimum of 14 weeks' maternity leave need not give notice of her intention to return.)

(vi) She must provide her employer with evidence of her EWC (or, if she is receiving SMP because she has already been confined, of her actual week of confinement) by the end of the third week of the Maternity Pay Period (MPP). If there is a good reason stopping her from producing evidence within this time limit, then the evidence can be submitted at any time up until the end of the 13th week of the MPP.

(b) *The Maternity Pay Period (MPP)*

SMP is not payable before the 11th week before the EWC unless the woman has been confined earlier, in which case it is paid in the week following confinement. It is paid on the employee's normal pay days or, if there are no 'normal pay days', on the last day of the month.

The MPP is a flexible period which starts not earlier than the 11th week before EWC nor later than the 6th week before EWC. It lasts for 18 weeks. The MPP may start at any time up to the 6th week before EWC if the woman continues in employment up to the end of the 7th week before EWC, without affecting her overall 18-week entitlement.

If she continues to work beyond the end of the 7th week before EWC then she will lose one week of SMP for each week during which she works (she will lose SMP at the lower rate before she loses any of her higher-rate entitlement). No SMP can be paid later than the 11th week after EWC.

(c) *Rates of SMP*

(i) There are two rates of SMP, the Lower Rate and the Higher Rate:

- *Higher-rate SMP* is 9/10 of the woman's 'normal weekly earnings' for the last eight weeks into the qualifying week. Higher-rate SMP is payable for the first six weeks of the Maternity Pay Period. Prior to 1994, higher-rate SMP was payable only to women who had completed two years' service by the 11th week before the EWC. The additional service requirement was removed by the Maternity Allowance and Statutory Maternity Pay Regulations 1994 (SI 1994 No. 1230).
- *Lower-rate SMP* is fixed by the Secretary of State for Employment. Once a woman's entitlement to higher-rate SMP is exhausted, the balance of her SMP entitlement is paid at the lower rate.

(ii) Originally, as with SSP, the whole of the employer's liability to pay SMP could be reclaimed from the State. Now employers can reclaim:

- in the case of a small employer (ie one whose total annual primary and secondary NI contributions do not exceed £20,000) all SMP plus an additional 5.5 per cent towards the cost of his NI contributions on the payments (see *Statutory Maternity Pay (Compensation of Employers) and Miscellaneous Amendment Regulations 1994 (SI 1994 No. 1882)*)
- in the case of any other employer 92 per cent of the cost of any SMP paid.

(iii) The amount of SMP that is reclaimable is reclaimed by deduction from the NI and income tax payments which would otherwise be payable for the period.

(e) *Normal weekly earnings*

A woman's normal weekly earnings are used for two purposes:

- First to calculate whether or not her earnings are above the NI Lower Earnings Limit (and hence whether or not she is entitled to receive SMP at all).
- Second, to calculate the woman's Higher-rate SMP entitlement. Normal weekly earnings are calculated as the woman's average weekly earnings over the eight weeks immediately preceding the 14th week before EWC.

Where a woman is paid monthly then her normal weekly earnings for this period are calculated as the sums that she has been paid in the relevant eight-week period divided by the number of months in respect of which she has been paid during that period multiplied by 12/52.

There is also a special definition of 'earnings' for SMP purposes. 'Earnings' are a woman's gross earnings and include any remuneration or profit derived from a woman's employment. Specifically, 'earnings' are taken to include and to exclude the following main items:

Inclusions:

- SSP, contractual sick pay (except for any amount that the woman has contributed towards her own sick pay) and any contractual payment made because of pregnancy or confinement
- certain sums paid under employment tribunal orders relating to unfair dismissal and redundancy claims

- where a woman is paid an annual bonus or some other such lump sum during the relevant eight-week period then this will generally form part of her 'earnings' for that period, and a payment of this type may greatly enhance her normal weekly earnings for SMP purposes.

Exclusions:
- any holiday pay where it is paid from a fund contributed to by more than one employer
- any payment in respect of a gratuity or offering which is not made by the employer
- any payment in kind or provision of board, lodgings or other services
- any pension payment
- any payment towards expenses incurred by a woman in travelling to her place of employment or training under the Disabled Persons (Employment) Act 1944
- a payment by way of, or derived from, shares apportioned under a statutorily approved profit-sharing scheme
- any VAT paid on goods or services supplied by the woman
- any redundancy payment
- any payment of, or contribution to, expenses incurred by the woman in carrying out her employment (where an 'allowance' is paid in respect of expenses then, if part of that allowance represents a profit in the woman's hands, that profit will be a part of her 'earnings').

(f) *Who is liable to pay?*

A woman's employer is liable to pay SMP, provided the woman meets all the conditions. An employer, for these purposes, is a person who is liable to pay Secondary Class 1 NI contributions in respect of the woman.

A woman cannot be asked to contribute to her own SMP except that SMP may be set off against any contractual maternity pay that is paid to her. Neither can any agreement be made to modify or exclude any terms of the SMP scheme. There is also provision for any employer who has dismissed an employee solely or mainly to avoid SMP liability to be made liable to pay the woman's SMP.

(g) *Exclusion and disqualification from SMP entitlement*

It should be noted that, unlike SSP, which deals with payments and disqualifications in units of 'days', SMP is dealt with in units of 'weeks'. A woman may lose her entitlement to SMP, or to a part of it, in any of the following circumstances:

    (i)   Working during the MPP

SMP is not payable for any week during which the employee works for her employer under a contract of employment.

If the woman works for another employer after her confinement during her MPP she ceases to be entitled to SMP for the remainder of the MPP. The woman is obliged to notify her 'liable' employer of any such employment within seven days of its starting. (Since most women are unlikely to know that they are under a duty to inform you if they work for someone else during the MPP, your Staff Handbook should make this clear.)

(ii) In legal custody

There is no liability to pay SMP for any week during which a woman is in legal custody or sentenced to a term of imprisonment (unless the sentence is suspended).

(iii) Death

If the woman dies during the MPP the employer's liability ends in the week following the week of her death.

(h) *The nature of SMP*

SMP, like SSP, is subject to income tax and NI deductions. There is also a right to make deductions from SMP in the same way and to the same extent as such deductions could be made from the woman's ordinary pay.

(i) *Records*

Employers must retain the following records for three years following the tax year in which the MPP ends:

(i) first notified day of absence in the MPP and the first day of the MPP if different (eg because of early confinement)

(ii) the weeks of the tax year in which SMP was paid and the amount paid in each week

(iii) any week in the tax year during an employee's MPP for which no payment was made to her, together with the reason why no payment was made

(iv) any medical evidence provided to the employer of the EWC or of the actual week of confinement. If the employer has returned this evidence to the woman for her to make any social security claims it is sufficient if he keeps a copy. If the medical evidence is of the actual week of confinement then the employer must keep a note of this. If the employee gives her employer the birth certificate then this must be returned to her.

(j) *Disputes*

Disputes about SMP liability are generally dealt with through the social security scheme rather than at employment tribunal, although the inclusion of SMP in the definition of 'wages' under the protection of wages provisions of the ERA means that an employer's failure to pay could be treated as an unlawful deduction and thus be amenable to litigation before an employment tribunal. If the employer fails to pay the woman, or fails to pay the correct amount, or fails to pay it at the right time, then he can be prosecuted under the social security legislation.

(k) *Special cases*

There are special rules that deal with cases where the employer has dismissed the employee to avoid SMP liability. In such cases the employee may, nonetheless, be able to claim SMP from him provided that she has been continuously employed for at least eight weeks.

If the woman is confined before the 14th week before EWC, she will be entitled to SMP, if she would otherwise have qualified for SMP. The position as it would otherwise have been at the 14th week before EWC may be difficult to judge, however, since form MAT-B 1, which specifies EWC, is not usually available until the 14th week before EWC.

93.3 Industrial injuries

(a) *Entitlement*

- An employee who is injured by an accident arising out of and in the course of his employment will be entitled to industrial injuries benefit.
- Where an accident occurs in the course of employment then there is a presumption that the accident also arose out of that employment unless the contrary is proven.
- An injury caused by an accident to an employee who is, with the employer's permission, travelling to or from work as a passenger in a vehicle provided by or under an arrangement with his employer, is taken to be an industrial injury.
- An injury caused by an accident to an employee in an emergency or supposed emergency, while the employee is on any premises where he is employed to work, is taken to be an industrial injury if he is trying to help people or save property.
- An injury to an employee that was not caused or contributed to by the employee's own misconduct is treated as an industrial injury if it:
  - arises out of another person's misconduct, skylarking or negligence
  - arises out of any steps taken in consequence of another person's misconduct, skylarking or negligence
  - arises out of the behaviour or presence of an animal (including a bird, fish or insect)
  - is caused by or consists of an employee being struck by an object or lightning.
- Employees who suffer from prescribed industrial diseases or prescribed personal injuries (which are not caused by accidents arising out of and in the course of their employment) can also claim industrial injuries benefit.

(b) *The benefit*

Industrial injuries benefit consists of:

(i) Disablement benefit

- Where the loss of mental or physical faculties arising out of the disablement is not less than 14 per cent (20 per cent where the claim was made before 1 October 1986) then the employee will be entitled to a disablement pension. In assessing the employee's disability level any pre-existing disability is taken into account as adding to the overall percentage of disability.
- A higher disability pension is payable where the level of disability is 100 per cent and constant attendance is needed.

(ii)   Reduced earnings allowance
       A reduced earnings allowance can be claimed in respect of an accident which happened before 1 October 1990 and which resulted in the employee being permanently disabled from following his normal occupation. Where the accident results in a diminution in the employee's earning capacity a reduced earnings allowance may be available to supplement the employee's earnings.
(iii) Retirement allowance
       Where a person who was entitled to a reduced earnings allowance retires then they may also be entitled to a retirement allowance that will top-up their normal pension to take into account their reduced earning capacity.
(iv)   Industrial death benefit
       Provides for a widow's benefit where a person dies who was entitled, or who but for their death would have been entitled, to claim in respect of an industrial injury.

93.4   Notional strike pay

Where an employee is on strike or has an interest in a trade dispute, a set amount of notional strike pay is to be taken into account in assessing any entitlement that he may have to social security benefits. This notional sum is taken into account in assessing the employee's entitlement to benefit whether or not he actually receives it.

94   Social Security (Incapacity for Work) Act 1994

Amends the Social Security Contributions and Benefits Act 1992 (SSCBA) and the Social Security Administration Act 1992.

The major thrust of this Act is to bring in a new way of assessing a person's ability or inability to work. This method of assessment is relevant only for benefits under the SSCBA itself and even then is expressly not applicable to assessment of inability for industrial injuries or SSP purposes. From an employment point of view it therefore has very little effect. Other employment-related provisions in the Act amend existing legislation and are dealt with in the relevant statutes.

95   Social Security (Medical Evidence, Claims and Payments) Amendment Regulations 1982

These regulations provide that medical practitioners need not give national health insurance certificates to cover the first seven calendar days when a person is ill.

95A   Social Security (Welfare to Work) Regulations 1998 (SI 1998 No. 2231)

Provide that where welfare to work beneficiaries have two periods of incapacity for work that are separated by less than 52 weeks, the two are to be treated as a single period of incapacity for work. The effect of this is that where welfare to work beneficiaries are taken into employment the State, rather than the employer, picks up the sick pay liability for such employees.

96 Statutory Sick Pay Act 1991 (repealed)

Amends Social Security and Housing Benefits Act 1982 and Social Security Acts 1985 and 1986.

Repealed and consolidated into the Social Security Contributions and Benefits Act 1992 and the Social Security Administration Act 1992.

97 Statutory Sick Pay Act 1994

Amends the Social Security Contributions and Benefits Act 1992 and the Social Security Administration Act 1992.

(a) *Removal of right to recoup SSP*

Under the original SSP scheme the employer was able to recoup 100 per cent of the SSP paid out to employees. Indeed, under the Social Security Act 1985, the principle of reimbursement was extended to allow the employer to reclaim a further amount in respect of the secondary Class 1 National Insurance contributions he was liable to pay on SSP payments.

From 6 April 1991, the Statutory Sick Pay Act 1991 provided that an employer could recoup only 80 per cent of the amount of SSP which he paid out, and removed the provision for reclaiming the allowance for secondary National Insurance contributions.

The Statutory Sick Pay Act 1994 removes the general right for employers to reclaim any SSP paid to employees after April 1995.

(b) *'Small employer's' relief (SER)*

SER was introduced by the Statutory Sick Pay Act 1991, to allow small employers to reclaim at least part of the amount they expended on SSP. The original scheme is replaced by a scheme made under the 1994 Act together with the Statutory Sick Pay Percentage Threshold Order 1995 (SI 1995/512), which came into effect in April 1995. The scheme allows employers to recoup SSP payments from the State to the extent that those payments exceed 13 per cent of the employer's NI contributions for the month in question. The level of 13 per cent was set to equate to the cost of the original SER.

98 Sunday Trading Act 1994 (repealed consolidated)

The provisions of Schedule 4 of this Act, which provide for the protection of shop workers in relation to Sunday work, have been repealed and consolidated into the Employment Rights Act 1996.

98A Teaching and Higher Education Act 1998

Amends the Employment Rights Act 1996 and provides a right to paid time off for young people to study or train.

(a) The right

LIVERPOOL JOHN MOORES UNIVERSITY
Aldham Roberts L.R.C.
TEL. 051 231 3701/3634

An employee who is:
- aged 16 or 17 (18 if the employee started the course before reaching 18)
- is not receiving full-time education; and
- has not attained certain specified standards of educational achievement

is entitled to have paid time off to undertake study or training leading to a relevant qualification.

(b) Time off can be taken whether the employee works directly for an employer or through an agency.

(c) The standards of educational achievement below which the employee can take time off for study under this provision are set down by the Right to Time Off for Study or Training Regulations 1999 (SI 1999 No. 986). Broadly the standards are:
- GCSEs: 5 grade A* to C
- SQA Standard Grades: 5 at grades 1 to 3
- one intermediate GNVQ or one GSVQ at level 2
- one NVQ or one SVQ at level 2
- one BTEC First Diploma awarded by the Edexel Foundation
- one BTEC First Certificate awarded by the Edexel Foundation
- City and Guilds of London Institute Diploma of Vocational Education at Intermediate Level; or
- 16 SQA unit or assessment credits at least eight of which are at Intermediate 2 or above and the remainder at Intermediate 1.

There are various provisions for lower qualification levels to be treated as part-qualifications for these purposes.

(d) The amount of time off to which an employee is entitled under these provisions and the occasions on which time off may be taken and any conditions subject to which it may be taken are those that are reasonable in all the circumstances having regard to:
- the requirements of the employee's study or training
- the circumstances of the employer's business (or the principal's business where the employee works through an employment agency); and
- the effect of the employee's time off on the running of that business.

(e) The employee can apply to an employment tribunal if he is refused time off or payment for time off. There is a three-month time limit for claiming, with the usual provision to extend time if it is not reasonably practicable for the claim to be brought within that time.

99 Trade Union Act 1913 (repealed consolidated)

Amended by Industrial Relations Act 1971, Trade Union and Labour Relations Act 1974, Employment Protection Act 1975, Employment Protection (Consolidation) Act 1978, Trade Union Act 1984 and Employment Act 1988 and 1990.

Its remaining provisions were consolidated into TULRA.

100 Trade Union Act 1984 (repealed consolidated)

Amends Employment Act 1980, Trade Union Act 1913, Trade Union and Labour Relations Act 1974. Amended by Employment Acts 1988 and 1990.

Its remaining provisions were consolidated into TULRA.

101 Trade Union (Amalgamations) Act 1964

Deals with the machinery under which trade unions can amalgamate and/or transfer their engagements.

This is repealed/consolidated into TULRA.

102 Trade Union and Labour Relations (Consolidation) Act 1992 (TULRA)

Consolidates the law relating to trade unions from the following statutes: Conspiracy and Protection of Property Act 1875, Trade Union Act 1913, Industrial Courts Act 1919, Trade Union (Amalgamations, etc.) Act 1964, Industrial Relations Act 1971, Trade Union and Labour Relations Act 1974, Trade Union and Labour Relations (Amendment) Act 1976, Employment Protection Act 1975, Employment Protection (Consolidation) Act 1978, Interpretation Act 1978, Reserve Forces Act 1980, Employment Acts 1980–1990, Trade Union Act 1984, Companies Consolidation (Consequential Provisions) Act 1985, Public Order Act 1986.

Amended by TURERA, Collective Redundancies and Transfer of Undertakings (Protection of Employment) (Amendment) Regulations SI 1995/2587, Employment Rights Act 1996, Employment Rights (Disputes Resolutions) Act 1998, Deregulation (Deduction from Pay of Union Subscriptions) Order 1998 and Transfer of Undertakings (Protection of Employment) (Amendment) Regulations 1999.

102.1 Meaning of 'trade union', list of unions and certification of independence

Originally ss 2, 8 and 30 Trade Union and Labour Relations Act 1974 and s 8 Employment Protection Act 1975.

(a) *Definition of 'trade union'*

A union is defined as:

    (i)   an organisation consisting of workers of one or more types whose main purposes include the regulation of relations between workers of that type and employers or employers' associations; or

    (ii)   an organisation whose members are trade unions (such as the TUC).

(b) *List of trade unions*

    (i)   The Certification Officer keeps a list of trade unions. Organisations wishing to be registered as trade unions can apply to the Certification Officer. They must provide him with:

- a copy of the rules of the organisation
- a list of its officers

- the address of its head or main office
- the name by which it is, or is to be, known; and
- the prescribed fee.

(ii)   If the Certification Officer is satisfied that the organisation is a trade union, that it has fulfilled the above requirements and is not using a name which belongs to, or which has been used by, another registered trade union, then he must enter it on to the list of trade unions.

(iii)   The Certification Officer also has certain powers to strike unions off the list he holds.

(c) *Independent trade unions*

(i)   The majority of employment law rights conferred on trade unions have been restricted to those unions that are independent. A trade union is defined as independent if:

- it is not under the domination or control of one or more employers or employers' associations; and
- it is not liable to interference by any employer/s or employers' associations (through the provision of financial or material support or other means tending towards such control).

(ii)   A trade union that is on the list of trade unions can apply to the Certification Officer for a certificate of independence.

(iii)   The Certification Officer can withdraw a union's certificate of independence if he is of the opinion that the union is no longer independent. If he does this, however, the union can appeal against his decision.

102.2   Status and property of trade unions

(a) *Status of trade unions*

Although trade unions are not corporate bodies they have power to make contracts and to sue and to be sued in their own right. Their objects, which might otherwise be considered to be void as being in restraint of trade (since, for example, their objects might include preventing people from working), are specifically declared by statute not to offend against the general common law principles outlawing agreements that are in restraint of trade.

(b) *Property of trade unions*

(i)   The property of trade unions must be vested in trustees. The trustees can be personally liable, and can be sued by individual members of the union, if they misuse union property.

(ii)   It is unlawful for a trade union to use any of its property to pay for any penalty imposed on a union member by a court. If a union does make any such payment then it is under an obligation to recoup it and an individual member is entitled to force the union to pursue recoupment.

(iii)   Death benefits

- Unions may pay sums of up to £5,000 on the death of a member.
- Members can nominate their beneficiaries under these provisions.

(c) *Liability in tort*

The liability of unions in tort is dealt with under industrial action (see below).

102.3   Trade union administration

(a) *Register of members*

Unions are required to keep an up-to-date register of their members, including their home or work addresses. Where the names on the register are required to be given to an outsider, such as a scrutineer in relation to elections for certain union offices, the union is required to impose a duty of confidentiality on that person as regards the information on the register. This requirement was brought in by TURERA.

(b) *Duty to supply rules*

Unions are required to supply any person with a copy of its rules either free of charge or on payment of a reasonable fee.

(c) *Accounting records*

  (i)   Unions are required to prepare accounts and to keep them available for inspection for six years. Union members can inspect any such accounts, with their accountants if desired, for the time for which they have been members of the union.

  (ii) Unions are required to appoint auditors and to send annual returns to the Certification Officer. At the same time as sending an annual return to the Certification Officer unions are required to send an annual statement to members – broadly similar to a company's annual return. This latter amendment was introduced by TURERA.

102.4   Elections for trade union officers

(a) *Who must be elected*

The president, general secretary and members of the executive of a union must be re-elected every five years. This does not apply to long-serving members of the executive who are within five years of retirement and who would otherwise be allowed by the union rules to stay on until retirement without being re-elected.

(b) *The election process*

  (i)   No union member may be unreasonably excluded from standing for election.

  (ii)   Each candidate is allowed to prepare an election address in his own words. The candidates' election addresses must be distributed by the union.

  (iii) The union must appoint an independent scrutineer to oversee the election.

  (iv)   Generally, each union member must be given the same right to vote, but the union is entitled to exclude certain categories, such as those who are unemployed or in arrears with their subscriptions, or to limit the vote to certain classes of member within the union (eg to those within a particular geographical location or to members of a particular trade).

(v)   Each eligible member has a right to vote in a secret postal ballot. The votes must be counted by an independent person (this is a TURERA amendment) and there must be a scrutineer's report produced saying that the scrutineer is satisfied with the way in which the election has been conducted. The results of the election cannot be published until the scrutineer's report has OK'd the election. The union must send a copy or inform all members of the terms of the scrutineer's report within three months of receiving it. By amendments added by TURERA, the scrutineer is also required to examine the union's register of members and to satisfy himself that it is accurate and up to date.

102.5   Use of funds for political objectives

(a) *Political fund resolution*

A union's funds cannot be used for political purposes, as defined by the Act, unless:

(i)   The union has adopted a political resolution. Such a resolution must be approved by a majority of those voting in a ballot and the political resolution must be re-balloted every 10 years.

(ii)   The union must make payments for political objectives out of a separate fund, from which members can be exempted from contributing.

(iii)   The union's rules regarding the use of funds for political purposes must be approved by the Certification Officer.

(b) *Members' contributions to political funds*

(i)   When a union adopts a political resolution it must tell its members of that fact. It must also tell them that they are entitled to be exempted from contributing to the political fund. They must be told that they can obtain an exemption notice, exempting them from political fund contributions from the union's Head Office or from the Certification Officer. Section 84 sets out a statutory form of exemption notice that can be used by members not wishing to contribute to the political fund.

(ii)   If an employee who has union subscriptions deducted from his pay under the check-off system is exempt from making political fund contributions and notifies his employer of this in writing then:

- the employer must not deduct political fund contributions from that employee's pay; and
- the employer must not refuse to make deductions under the check-off system in respect of the employee while he continues to make check-off deductions for other employees (unless his refusal has nothing to do with the fact that the employee is exempt from making political fund contributions).

(iii)   Where the employer either:

- makes deductions despite the employee being exempt from contributing to the political fund; or
- refuses to continue to make deductions of the employee's union sub-

scriptions after being notified that the employee is exempt from contributing to the union's political fund

the employee can apply to the county court (sheriff's court in Scotland) which can make a declaration if it finds for the employee.

(iv) If the employee's complaint is that the employer has made unlawful deductions from his pay – by making deductions in respect of the political fund contribution when the employee was exempt – the time for bringing a claim under the s 23 ERA (claim for unlawful deductions from wages) runs from the date of the declaration by the court of the employee's right not to have had that amount deducted.

102.6   Funding and use of employer's premises for ballots

TULRA originally provided that public funding would be available for certain trade union ballots, including those for elections of the executive committee, political fund ballots and industrial action ballots. These provisions were repealed by TURERA with effect from 1 April 1996. The provisions allowing for the unions to use the employer's premises to hold such ballots where the employer recognised the union and had more than 20 employees was also repealed by TURERA with effect from 1 April 1996. To a large extent using the employer's premises would be of no assistance now since most types of ballot now require a postal rather than a workplace ballot.

102.7   Employers' Associations

The Act defines Employers' Associations, provides for the Certification Officer to keep a list of them, deals with the status and property of Employers' Associations and their administration, ability to apply funds for political objectives and for amalgamations and similar matters.

102.8   Rights of trade union members against the union

(a) *Rights on unballoted union action*

TULRA allows a trade union member to bring an action against the union where the union has authorised or endorsed any industrial action which has not been approved by a secret ballot. A member can bring an action only if members of the union (including the complainant himself) have been or are likely to be induced to take part in, or to continue, the 'unapproved' industrial action.

This provision gives individual union members the right to complain that the trade union has failed to hold a proper ballot or to obtain a vote in favour of the industrial action as a result of that ballot (see *Industrial action* below). Originally only employers were in a position to complain about a union's failure to obtain the sanction of a ballot before taking industrial action. This extension, to allow individual trade union members to complain of unballoted strike action, was originally brought into effect by the Employment Act 1988.

(b) *Access to the courts for members*

Where a trade union member has applied for any matter to be determined in accordance with the trade union's rules and that matter has not been dealt with within six months, then, regardless of anything in the union rules, the member can take his grievance to court. There are provisions which allow this six-month period to be extended where the reason for the union failing to deal with the issue was the member's own fault.

If the individual's application to the union to deal with any matter is invalid then the union must inform him, within 28 days of the application, of the ways in which the application is invalid. If the union fails to do this then the member is entitled to treat his application as validly made.

(c) *Right not to be unjustifiably disciplined*

A trade union member/former member is given the right not to be unjustifiably disciplined by the union. It is unjustifiable for a union to discipline someone because he is or is believed to be guilty of any of the following:

(i)   not supporting, or indicating opposition to, or lack of support for, a strike or other industrial action

(ii)   not breaching an agreement between himself and his employer to support a strike or other industrial action (NB The wording of this makes it clear that this is not limited to employees who are trade union members.)

(iii)   asserting, or vindicating someone else's assertion, that the union or any official or representative of the union or a trustee of any union property has contravened or proposes to contravene any agreement, union rule or rule of law, or consulting the Certification Officer in respect of any such matter – unless the member is acting in bad faith in making or vindicating an assertion which he believes to be false

(iv)   encouraging or helping someone else not to breach his agreement with his employer

(v)   failing to agree to, or withdrawing agreement from, deductions being made from his wages in respect of union dues

(vi)   resigning, or proposing to resign, from a union, becoming, or proposing to become, a member of another union or refusing to become a member of another union

(vii)   working with, or proposing to work with, non-union members

(viii) working for, or proposing to work for, an employer who employs or who has employed non-union members, whether of the particular union or of another union; or

(ix)   requiring the union to do anything that the union is required by TULRA to do if asked by a member.

Unjustifiable discipline in this context includes:

- expulsion, from the union or from a branch of it
- a fine of any sort
- withdrawal of any of the services or benefits of membership
- any other detriment.

Complaints under these provisions must be presented to an employment tribunal within three months of the decision which gave rise to the complaint.

If the tribunal finds the complaint well founded it will make a declaration to that effect. The applicant can then apply to the tribunal if the union's decision has been withdrawn and it has done all it can to ensure a reversal of the effects of that decision or to the Employment Appeals Tribunal (EAT) if those steps have not been taken.

Any such application cannot be made earlier than four weeks after the tribunal's declaration. In these, later, proceedings the tribunal or EAT can:

- order repayment of any sums the member has paid out under the union's decision; and
- award such compensation as it considers 'just and equitable in all the circumstances of the case', subject to the total not exceeding the maximum basic award plus the maximum compensatory award that could be obtained in an unfair dismissal case (see *Employment Rights Act 1996* – unfair dismissal remedies).

(d) *Right to terminate union membership*

Every union member has the right to terminate his union membership on giving reasonable notice and complying with any reasonable conditions.

(e) *Right not to be excluded or expelled from union*

The Employment Act 1980 provided a right for employees who were in 'closed shop' employment not to be unreasonably expelled or excluded from the trade unions that were party to the closed shop agreement. (A 'closed shop' meant that only members of the appropriate unions could be employed in that employment.) TURERA has extended this protection, in modified form, to protect all trade union members and would-be trade union members from being excluded from or expelled by a trade union, other than on certain specific grounds.

(i) The right

The grounds on which a person can be excluded or expelled from a trade union are:

- if the person no longer meets an 'enforceable membership requirement'. An 'enforceable membership requirement' is one that restricts membership by reference purely to:
  - employment in a specified trade, industry or profession
  - occupational description (including grade, level or category of appointment); or
  - possession of specific trade, industrial or professional qualifications or work experience
- if the person is not within the geographical area in which the union operates
- where the union operates within a single company or within a group of

associated companies, if the person ceases to be employed by the company/group
- where the exclusion or expulsion is solely because of the individual's conduct. But there are certain types of conduct for which it is not permissible to expel or exclude an individual. These are:
  - the individual being or ceasing to be
    - a member of another trade union
    - employed by a particular employer or at a particular place, or
    - a member of a political party, or
  - conduct in relation to any trade union for which, under the Act (see (c) above), an individual may not be disciplined by a trade union.

(ii) Remedies
- A complaint may be made to a tribunal within six months of the date of expulsion or exclusion from the union or, if that is not reasonably practicable, within such further time as is reasonably practicable.
- Where the tribunal finds the claim to be substantiated it must make a declaration to that effect.
- Compensation:
  - If the employee is admitted/re-admitted by the union, then the compensation claim is heard by an employment tribunal, otherwise the claim is dealt with by the EAT.
  - The claim, in either case, must be made within four weeks of the tribunal's declaration.
  - The amount of compensation awarded is such as is considered just and equitable and a reduction can be made for any contributory conduct on the part of the applicant.
  - The maximum award that can be made is:
    - 30 weeks' pay (subject to the statutory upper limit for a 'week's pay'); plus
    - the maximum compensatory award for unfair dismissal.
    Where the EAT makes the award, the minimum award is £5,000 (and this appears, from the wording of the section, to be after any reduction for contributory fault has been taken into account).

(f) *Commissioner for the Rights of Trade Union Members*
This post was abolished by the Employment Relations Act 1999, but some of the functions have effectively been taken over by the Certification Officer under other provisions of that Act.

102.9   Rights of trade union members in relation to employment

(a) *Right to require the employer to stop deductions of union subscriptions*
A more extensive right was substituted by TURERA. The original requirement (in the 1992 Act) was that if an employee informed his employer that he had left the union with effect from a particular date then the employer must stop checking off union dues from that date or as soon thereafter as is

reasonably practicable. TURERA introduced a rather more onerous set of requirements for employers and employees to comply with if check-off was to apply. This included a requirement that the employee's authorisation for the employer to continue the check-off arrangement in his case should be renewed every three years. The Deregulation (Deduction from Pay of Union Subscriptions) Order 1998 allows employers to send a notice to employees (in a form laid down in the Order). These notices ask employees to write back and make a positive election if they wish to limit to the original three-year period their authorisation for their union dues to be checked off. If they do not write back to the employer within 14 days, the original authorisation is to be treated as continuing until it is specifically withdrawn by the employee. The requirement for employers to give employees a month's notice of any change in subscription levels is also removed. Apart from these amendments:

(i) The right requires an employer:
  - not to make any union subscription deduction which is not authorised; and
  - to ensure that any subscription deduction that is made is not more than the authorised amount.

(ii) To be authorised, permission to make the subscription deduction must be authorised in a written document which is:
  - signed and dated by the worker;
  - subject to what is said above, no more than three years old at the date when the deduction is made.
  - Where the authorisation has been withdrawn then no deductions may be made after the withdrawal has been received by the employer (subject to there being enough time after the date of the withdrawal for it to be reasonably practicable to stop the deductions being made from the payment in question).

(iii) An employee can complain to an employment tribunal that an employer has made unauthorised or excessive deductions, within three months of the deduction in question or, where that is not reasonably practicable, within such further time as is reasonably practicable.

(iv) Nothing in these arrangements, however, requires an employer to deduct union subscriptions from an employee's pay for the union if he does not wish to do so.

(iv) (For the right of union members not to have unauthorised political fund contributions deducted from their pay and for their right to continue to have the remainder of their union subscriptions deducted by the employer after they have elected not to contribute to the political fund see *Use of funds for political objectives* above, Section 102.5.)

(b) *Discriminatory recruitment on 'trade union grounds'*
  (i) Refusing employment

- The Act provides that it is unlawful for a person to be refused employment on 'trade union grounds'. This makes it unlawful for an employer to refuse to employ a person because either:
  - he is or is not a member of a trade union
  - he is unwilling to accept a requirement to remain, or to become, or to cease to be, a union member; or
  - he refuses to have money deducted from his pay as an alternative to being a union member, etc.
- Where there is an arrangement whereby employment is offered only to people put forward by a trade union, then an applicant who applies for and is refused employment because of this practice is deemed to have been refused employment on trade union grounds.
- The Act contains an extended definition of 'refusing employment', which includes:
  - failing to entertain the applicant's application or enquiry, or causing him to withdraw it
  - refusing to offer the applicant employment
  - offering the job on terms which no one who wanted to fill the post would offer
  - offering it on condition that the employee must meet the 'trade union' requirement (eg by joining or leaving the union); or
  - offering the job and then withdrawing that offer.

(ii) Discriminatory advertising

Where an advertisement is published which indicates, or which might reasonably be understood as indicating, that the employer will require the successful applicant to be or to become a trade union member or to cease to be one, then an employee who applies for and is refused employment is conclusively presumed to have been refused employment on trade union grounds if:

- he either does not meet that requirement; or
- he is unwilling to accept that requirement.

This is particularly stringent since it imposes strict liability on an employer in such cases.

(iii) Discrimination by an employment agency

There are provisions equivalent to items (i) and (ii) above relating to employment agencies. These make it unlawful for an employment agency either to refuse to offer its services on trade union grounds, or to publish a discriminatory advertisement.

For these purposes a trade union is not to be considered as an employment agency in relation to services provided for its members.

(iv) Union membership requirements in contracts for supply of goods or services

- Any term or condition in a contract for the supply of goods or services which requires the work to be carried out by union members is declared void. Similarly, any term which requires an employer to recognise, consult with or negotiate with a trade union is also void.

- It is unlawful to refuse to deal with any supplier of goods or services on grounds relating to the trade union status of any of that supplier's employees. It is also unlawful to refuse to deal with a supplier on the grounds that they recognise, consult or negotiate with a trade union (or because they do not do so).

(v) Remedy
  - Time limit

A complaint may be made to an employment tribunal within three months of the discrimination in question. The type of case where problems can immediately be envisaged, in terms of trying to determine when the discrimination actually occurred, is where an employer has simply omitted to offer employment. In such a case the Act provides that time for application is to run from 'the end of the period within which it was reasonable to expect the employer to act'. This may lead to some interesting case law.

  - Remedies

The employment tribunal can order the employer to pay compensation, which is to be assessed in the same way as compensation for breach of statutory duty (and which can include compensation for injury to feelings). The maximum amount of compensation that can be awarded is the same as the maximum unfair dismissal compensatory award (set at £50,000 by the Redundant Relations Act 1999 with effect from 25 October 1999 and index linked thereafter).

In addition to a monetary award, the tribunal can recommend that the respondent take specific action to obviate or reduce the adverse effect on the applicant of the conduct complained of. If the respondent fails to take the recommended action the tribunal can award compensation, or greater compensation to reflect that failure. The total award, however, is still subject to the same overall maximum as the maximum unfair dismissal compensation.

  - Joinder of third parties

Where the employer's conduct was to any extent caused by a third party exercising pressure by threatening to call a strike or to take other industrial action, that third party (which will usually be a trade union) can be joined to the proceedings. In such cases the tribunal can make a compensatory award against either or both parties and in such proportions as it sees fit. Where the case could be brought against an employer or an employment agency and the union member takes action against only one then the other can be joined at the instance of either party and any compensation can again be awarded against either or both in such proportions as the tribunal considers just in the circumstances.

(c) *Subjection to a detriment*

The original terms of the Act that protected employees against 'action short of dismissal' on union grounds were changed by the Employment Relations Act

1999 to a prohibition against subjecting an individual to detriment on union grounds.

(i)   The prohibition

An employer is not allowed to subject the employee to a detriment by any act or failure to act:

- to prevent or deter him from, or to penalise him for:
    - being a member of an independent trade union; or
    - taking part, at an appropriate time, in the activities of an independent trade union. (An 'appropriate time' for taking part in trade union activities for these purposes is outside working hours or during working hours at times when by agreement or arrangement with the employer it is permissible to take part in union activities.)
- to compel him to be a member of a trade union
- to enforce a requirement to pay an amount in lieu of union dues for non-union members.

(ii)   Exclusion for personal contracts

Where an employee is offered an inducement to enter into a personal contract (ie to enter into a separately negotiated agreement with his employer rather than accepting the terms that have been collectively agreed with the union) then this is expressly declared by statute not to be action short of dismissal against a person who does not accept this inducement (unless no employer could reasonably use the inducement in question to try to change his contractual relationship with his employees – for example, offering to pay non-union members double what was negotiated with the union under the collective agreement). This amendment was brought in by TURERA, although the cases which it was introduced to overrule have since been overruled by the House of Lords on appeal.

(iii) Remedy

An employee can bring a claim at any time within three months of the action in question (with a provision to extend this time limit if it cannot reasonably be met). Where there is a series of actions giving rise to the complaint then it is from the last that the three-month time limit runs.

No account is to be taken of any pressure placed on the employer to take the action complained of. Any third party can be joined to the proceedings, and the tribunal can make an award against the third party to the extent that is just and equitable.

(d) *Dismissal for trade union reasons*

(i)   The prohibition

The dismissal or selection for redundancy of an employee on grounds of trade union membership or taking part in trade union activities is to be regarded as unfair. Such dismissals are considered to be for an inadmissible reason. Inadmissible reasons for dismissal are:

- because the employee was, or proposed to become, a member of an independent trade union

- because the employee had taken part, or proposed to take part, in the activities of an independent trade union at an appropriate time (an 'appropriate time' for taking part in trade union activities for these purposes is outside working hours or during working hours at times when by agreement or arrangement with the employer it is permissible to take part in union activities); or
- because he was not a member of a union or of a particular trade union
- because he refused to agree to allow his employer to deduct an amount in lieu of union dues from his pay.

(ii) Remedies

The remedies in a case of unfair dismissal, or unfair selection for redundancy on grounds of trade union membership or activities, are the same as those for 'special cases' of unfair dismissal under ERA; both have been modified by Employment Relations Act 1999. There is also a facility to join third parties to proceedings and a provision for interim relief to be provided to allow for the contract of employment to be continued pending the outcome of the tribunal case (see also *ERA: Protection for health and safety representatives, trustees of pension schemes and employee representatives* above, Section 36.6, where these remedies are dealt with in more detail).

(e) *Time off for trade union duties*

(i) The right

- An employee who is an official of a recognised independent trade union is entitled not to be unreasonably refused paid time off during working hours for:
  - negotiations with the employer about:
    - things falling within the statutory definition of collective bargaining (see *Industrial relations, collective bargaining* below)
    - in respect of the which the union is recognised by the employer
  - the performance of functions which the employer has agreed may be performed by the union related to
    - things falling within the statutory definition of collective bargaining (see *Industrial relations, collective bargaining* below)
    - in respect of the which the union is recognised by the employer
  - training to enable the official to carry out the above duties, provided that the training is approved by the TUC or by the independent trade union of which he is an official.
- The amount of time off which is to be permitted and the reasons for it are subject to what is reasonable and to the terms of an ACAS Code of Practice.

(ii) Remedy

A trade union official who is unreasonably refused paid time off or who is not paid for it can complain to an employment tribunal within three months of the incident, or within such further time as is reasonably practicable if it is not reasonably practicable to meet the three-month time limit. Where the tribunal finds that the official has not been paid where he should have been, it must award payment for time off which should have been given; it may also award compensation for the failure to give time off.

(f) *Time off for trade union activities*

   (i)   The right

- An employee who is a member of a recognised independent trade union is entitled to reasonable time off during working hours to take part in:
  - any activities of the union; and
  - any activities of the union in relation to which he is an official or representative of the union.
- The amount of time off that is to be permitted and the reasons for it are subject to what is reasonable and to the terms of an ACAS Code of Practice.

   (ii)   Remedy

A trade union member who is unreasonably refused time off for trade union activities can complain to an employment tribunal within three months of the incident, or within such further time as is reasonably practicable if it is not reasonably practicable to meet the three-month time limit. On an application the tribunal may make an award of compensation for time off which should have been given.

102.10   Procedure for handling redundancies

Until 1995 the right to have representatives consulted in relation to redundancies would have been seen as a right accorded to trade union members. TURERA and the Collective Redundancies and Transfer of Undertakings (Protection of Employment) (Amendment) Regulations 1995 SI 1995/2587, which were brought in to give effect to requirements under Council Directive 92/56/EEC and to deal with the shortfall in the way in which the UK had dealt with its original obligations in respect of collective redundancies under Council Directive 75/129/EEC (the Collective Redundancies Directives), have had the effect of extending these provisions both in relation to when and how consultation must occur and in terms of requiring consultation where unions are not recognised.

(a) *Extended meaning of redundancy for consultation purposes and presumption of redundancy*

For purposes of the consultation requirements, 'dismissal for redundancy' is widely defined as meaning dismissal for a reason or reasons not related to the individual concerned. It is presumed that any proposal to dismiss an employee is because of redundancy, in this extended sense, unless the employer shows the dismissal to be for some other reason.

(b) *Consultation* (This section has been considerably amended by the Collective Redundancies and Transfer of Undertakings (Protection of Employment) (Amendment) Regulations 1999 (SI 1999 No. 1925) (*qv*))

(i) Circumstances in which required, and timing
  - Where an employer is proposing to dismiss 20 or more employees at one establishment within a period of 90 days or less, then he must consult with the appropriate representative of all employees affected by the proposed redundancies or who may be affected by measures taken in connection with those dismissals at least 30 days before the first dismissal takes effect. (This provision was amended by the Collective Redundancies and Transfer of Undertakings (Protection of Employment) (Amendment) Regulations 1999 (SI 1999 No. 1925) (*qv*))
  - Where the employer is proposing to dismiss more than 100 employees at one establishment within a period of 90 days, then he must start consultations at least 90 days before the first dismissal takes effect.
  - In considering the numbers of employees being dismissed, no account is to be taken of employees in respect of whom consultation has already begun.
  - These provisions do not apply to those who are employed:
    - under a contract for a fixed term of three months or less, or
    - under a contract to perform a specific task which is not expected to last for more than three months, provided that the employee/s in question have not been continuously employed for more than three months.
  - Where there are special circumstances that make it not reasonably practicable for the employer to start consultations with employee representatives on time, then he must do what he can towards meeting these requirements. (It is no excuse if the employer's decision to make redundancies has been taken by someone who controls the employer (such as a holding company) and that person has not given the employer information that he needs to start consultations.)
(ii) Employee representatives
  - The provisions relating to election of employee representatives were fundamentally changed by the Collective Redundancies and Transfer of Undertakings (Protection of Employment) (Amendment) Regulations 1999 (SI 1999 No. 1925) (*qv*).
  - An employer must allow employee representatives:
    - access to the employees who are affected by the redundancy; and
    - accommodation and such other facilities as may be appropriate.
(iii) Starting consultation
  - To begin consultation, the employer must disclose the following matters in writing to the appropriate representatives:
    - the reasons for his proposals
    - the numbers and descriptions of employees whom it is proposed to dismiss as redundant
    - the total number of employees of any such description employed by the employer at the establishment in question

- the proposed method of selecting the employees who may be dismissed
- the proposed method of carrying out the dismissals, with due regard to any agreed procedure, including the period over which the dismissals are to take effect; and
- the proposed method of calculating the amount of any redundancy payments in excess of the statutory which are to be made to those who are made redundant.
- The above information must be given to appropriate representatives directly or sent by post.
- The employer must also provide employee representatives with a copy of any notice that the employer is required to give to the Secretary of State regarding the redundancies (see (d) below).
- Where there are special circumstances that make it not reasonably practicable for the employer to give the employee representatives this information, or to give it to them on time, then he must do what he can towards meeting these requirements. It is no excuse if the employer's decision to make redundancies has been taken by someone who controls the employer (such as a holding company) and that person has not given the employer any of the information he needs for these purposes.

(iv) What consultation involves

- Consultation must be undertaken by the employer with a view to reaching agreement with the appropriate representatives on matters including ways of:
  - avoiding the dismissals
  - reducing the numbers of employees to be dismissed; and
  - mitigating the consequences of the dismissals.
- Where there are special circumstances that make it not reasonably practicable to fulfil these requirements then the employer must do what he can towards meeting them. (It is no excuse if the employer's decision to make redundancies has been taken by someone who controls the employer (such as a holding company) and that person has failed to provide the employer with any information he may require.)

(c) *Protective award*

(i) Protective award

- A protective award is made in respect of:
  - employees who have been dismissed, or whom it is proposed to dismiss, as redundant; and
  - in respect of whom the consultation requirements have not been fully complied with.

The order requires the employer to pay the employees their remuneration during the protected period. (Employees who are employed during the protective period are entitled to remuneration only if they are entitled

to it under their contracts or if they are entitled to it as payment for their statutory notice period under the ERA.)
- The protected period begins with the earlier of:
  - the date on which the first of the dismissals takes effect; or
  - the date of the award.

  The protected period continues for such time as the tribunal considers just and equitable having regard to the seriousness of the employer's default, but can be no longer than 90 days (the erstwhile lower limit of 30 days for cases where between 30 and 100 employees were made redundant has been removed by the Collective Redundancies and Transfer of Undertakings (Protection of Employment) (Amendment) Regulations 1999 (SI 1999 No. 1925)).
- Where an employee is entitled to be paid under a protective award and the employer fails to pay then the employee can bring a claim to an employment tribunal within three months of that failure, or such longer time as is reasonably practicable, where it is not reasonably practicable to meet the three-month limit.

(ii) Who may claim a protective award and when (This area has been significantly altered by the Collective Redundancies and Transfer of Undertakings (Protection of Employment) (Amendment) Regulations 1999 (SI 1999 No. 1925))
- The appropriate claimant where an employer has not fulfilled the consultation requirements depends on the employer's particular failure, and will be:
  - in the case of any failure relating to election of employee representatives, any of the affected employees or any of the employees who have been dismissed as redundant
  - in the case of any other failure relating to employee representatives, the employee representatives to whom the failure relates
  - in the case of any failure to fulfil any requirement relating to a trade union representative, the trade union
  - in any other case, an affected employee or one who has been or may be dismissed as redundant.
- The burden of proof is put on the employer in two cases:
  - if the question arises as to whether or not the employee representative was appropriate, the employer must prove that the employee representative had authority to represent the affected employees; and
  - it is for the employer to prove that the requirements concerning the election of employee representatives have been complied with.
- A claim must be brought either:
  - before the last dismissal to which the claim relates; or
  - within three months of the last dismissal (or if that is not reasonably practicable, within such further period as is reasonably practicable).

- If the tribunal finds the claim to be well founded then it must make a declaration to that effect. It may also make a protective award.
  (iii) Termination of employment during the protected period
- If the employee is fairly dismissed (other than for redundancy) or unreasonably terminates his employment during the protective period then his right to be paid under the protective award ceases when his employment ends.
- Where an employee is offered suitable alternative employment while still employed he will lose his right to be paid under the protective award if he unreasonably refuses the offer. His entitlement to be paid under the protective award will cease from the time when the alternative employment would have started and he is, instead, dismissed or leaves.
- An employee who takes alternative employment on a trial basis and unreasonably terminates his employment during the trial period will lose his right to be paid under the protective award from the time when his employment ends.

(d) *Notifying the Secretary of State of redundancies*
- Where the employer is proposing to dismiss more than 100 employees at one establishment within a period of 90 days then he must notify the Secretary of State of his proposals at least 90 days before the first dismissal takes effect.
- Where an employer is proposing to dismiss between 20 and 100 employees at one establishment within a period of 90 days then he must notify the Secretary of State of his proposals at least 30 days before the first dismissal takes effect.
- In considering the numbers of employees being dismissed, no account is taken of employees in respect of whom a notice has already been given to the Secretary of State.
- A notice under this requirement must be in a form specified by the Secretary of State, and after receiving it the Secretary of State can ask for such further information as he may require.
- Where there are special circumstances that make it not reasonably practicable for the employer to notify the Secretary of State on time then he must do what he can towards meetings these requirements. (It is no excuse if the employer's decision to make redundancies has been taken by someone who controls the employer (such as a holding company) and that person has not given the employer information which he needs to notify the Secretary of State.)
- It is an offence to fail to notify the Secretary of State, or to fail to notify him on time. The company and any manager, officer or secretary responsible can be convicted of the failure.

(e) *Collective agreements*
- Where there is a collective agreement in force which establishes

- agreements for providing alternative employment for employees if they are dismissed as redundant; or
- arrangements for handling the dismissal of employees as redundant if the terms of the agreement are at least as beneficial to employees as the statutory consultation provisions then the parties can apply to the Secretary of State to be exempted from the statutory consultation requirements.

102.11   Collective bargaining

(a) *Collective agreements*
  (i)   Definitions
- A 'collective agreement' is an agreement about any matter that can be the subject of collective bargaining (see below). To be a collective agreement, the agreement must be reached between trade union/s and employer/s or employers' associations.
- 'Collective bargaining' means negotiations relating to or connected with one or more of the following:
  - terms and conditions of employment
  - physical conditions in which any workers are required to work
  - engagement/non-engagement, termination or suspension
    - of employment; or
    - of the duties of employment of one or more workers
  - allocation of work or the duties of employment between workers or groups of workers
  - matters of discipline
  - a worker's membership or non-membership of a trade union
  - facilities for officials of trade unions
  - machinery for negotiation or consultation
  - other procedures, relating to any of the above matters, including recognition by an employer of the right of a trade union to represent workers in such negotiations or consultation or in the carrying out of such procedures.
- 'Recognition' means recognition to any extent for collective bargaining purposes.
- 'Trade dispute' has two separate meanings – one for purposes of collective bargaining and the duties of ACAS, which is considerably wider than the second, which is used for purposes of deciding whether or not a trade union is immune from action in tort in respect of industrial action taken by its members. Both of these definitions are dealt with below, the first under 'Arbitration, mediation and conciliation' and the second under 'Industrial action'.
  (ii) Legal enforceability
- A collective agreement is conclusively presumed not to be legally binding unless:

- it contains a provision, however expressed, saying that the parties intend it to be legally enforceable; and
- it is in writing.
- A term in a collective agreement which prohibits or restricts the right of workers to take strike or other industrial action cannot form part of the worker's contract of employment unless the following conditions are met:
  - The collective agreement must:
    - be in writing
    - expressly say that those terms can be incorporated into the worker's contract
    - be reasonably accessible at the worker's place of work for him to consult during working hours; and
    - be one where each trade union that is a party to the agreement is an independent trade union; and
    - the worker's contract must expressly or impliedly incorporate those terms of the collective agreement.
  - Where the above criteria are met then the 'no strike' provisions take effect, notwithstanding:
    - the general proposition that collective agreements are unenforceable; and
    - despite any provision to the contrary in any agreement (including a collective agreement or a contract with any worker).

    NB: even if a 'no-strike' agreement is enforceable, an employee still cannot be forced by a court either to work or to attend at any place to do any work. The employer's only remedy against the employee will be in damages or to dismiss the employee.
- (b) *Disclosure of information for collective bargaining*
  - (i) General requirement
    - An employer who recognises an independent trade union must disclose information to that union's representatives, if they ask for it. The trade union representatives can request information for purposes of collective bargaining about matters for which the union is recognised by the employer. Subject to this, the types of information that may be requested are:
      - information without which the trade union representatives would be materially hampered in their collective bargaining with the employer, and
      - those which it would be good industrial relations practice for the employer to disclose to them for collective bargaining purposes.
    - When considering what it is 'good industrial relations practice to disclose' the provisions of the ACAS Code of Practice on Disclosure of Information must be taken into account, but not to the exclusion of any other evidence of what is good practice.

- The employer can ask for the union's request for disclosure to be in writing, or to be confirmed in writing, and the union can ask for the information to be in writing, or to be confirmed in writing.

(ii) Limitations on duty of disclosure
- An employer is not required to disclose information for collective bargaining purposes:
  - where disclosure would be against the interests of national security
  - which he could not disclose without contravening a statutory prohibition
  - which has been communicated to him in confidence, or obtained as a result of a confidence being entrusted to him by another person
  - which relates specifically to an individual (unless that individual has consented to its being disclosed)
  - where disclosure would cause substantial injury to the employer's undertaking for reasons other than its effect on collective bargaining
  - where the information was obtained by the employer for the purpose of bringing, prosecuting or defending any legal proceedings.
- Nor is an employer required:
  - to produce, make copies, or allow inspection of any document (other than a document prepared for the purpose of conveying or confirming the information)
  - to compile or assemble any information where the cost or work involved in compiling or assembling that information would be out of reasonable proportion to the value of the information in collective bargaining terms.

(iii) Complaints of failure to disclose
- A trade union can complain to the Central Arbitration Committee (CAC) that:
  - an employer has failed to disclose collective bargaining information; or
  - has failed to confirm that information in writing.
- The CAC refers such cases to ACAS for conciliation where possible or, if conciliation is not possible or has failed, the CAC hears the case. Where the CAC determines the case in favour of the union then it must make a declaration and give the employer a date not less than a week later by which the employer must disclose the information or in which to confirm the disclosed information in writing.
- If the employer fails to comply with the CAC's decision, the union can put in a further claim and can ask the CAC to make an award modifying the terms and conditions of relevant employees. The CAC can, on hearing the matter, award the terms and conditions claimed, or such other terms and conditions as it considers appropriate.

(c) *Codes of practice*
- ACAS can issue Codes of Practice containing practical guidance aimed at improving industrial relations.
- The Secretary of State may issue Codes of Practice containing practical guidance aimed at:
    - improving industrial relations, or
    - promoting good practice in relation to the way in which trade unions conduct ballots and elections.
- Any failure to follow any of these Codes of Practice does not give rise to any liability in itself, but may be taken into account by a tribunal, court or CAC as evidence in any case.

(d) *Arbitration, mediation and conciliation*
  (i)   ACAS
- Under an amendment made by TURERA, ACAS can offer advice to workers, employers and trade unions, or may publish advice on industrial relations issues. ACAS, under the TURERA amendments, is now also able to charge for its advice. ACAS's erstwhile 'general duty' to promote the improvement of industrial relations, particularly by helping to settle trade disputes, was removed by Employment Relations Act 1999.
- Where there is a trade dispute, ACAS can at the request of either party offer conciliation or mediation by an independent third party.
- Where there is a trade dispute, ACAS can at the request of one of the parties and with the consent of all of the parties, refer the matter to arbitration by arbitrators appointed by ACAS or by the CAC. Arbitration should not normally be used unless it is felt that conciliation will not work.
- ACAS can also involve itself in inquiries into industrial relations generally, or in relation to any particular industry where it sees fit to do so.

  (ii)   Courts of inquiry
- Where a trade dispute exists or is expected, a Court of Inquiry can be set up by the Secretary of State to look into it.

  (iii) Trade dispute
- A 'trade dispute' is defined more widely for purposes of the duties of ACAS in relation to trade disputes than it is for the part of the Act that deals with industrial action (see 102.12(b) below). For purposes of the duties of ACAS the definition of 'trade dispute':
    - includes a dispute between different sets of workers
    - includes a dispute between workers and any employer
    - includes disputes arising solely outside the UK which have no impact on those taking action in the UK
    - includes disputes involving unions and employers' associations
    - but does not include the mere threat of industrial action which is given in to by the party who or which was threatened.

102.12   Industrial action

(a) *Liability of trade unions in tort*

  (i) General

- A trade union can be liable in tort only if the action in question is one that is taken to have been authorised or endorsed by the trade union.
- An act is taken to have been authorised or endorsed by a trade union if it was done, authorised or endorsed:
  - by a person who is empowered by the union's rules to do, authorise or endorse acts of that kind, or
  - by the principal executive committee, the president or general secretary, or
  - by any other committee of the union, or
  - by any other official of the union who is part of a group whose duties or functions involve organising or co-ordinating industrial action.

  In relation to the last two groups above, an act is not to be taken as having been authorised or endorsed by virtue of these provisions if it is repudiated by the president, general secretary or executive committee of the union as soon as is reasonably practicable after it comes to the knowledge of any of them.

  (ii) Repudiating an action

To repudiate an act:

- written notice must be given to the offending committee or official without delay; and
- the union must give a written notice to all those whom they believe are taking part, or might otherwise take part in industrial action because of the act being repudiated. The notice must contain:
  - the fact of repudiation
  - the date of the repudiation; and
  - the following statement:

    > Your union has repudiated the call (or calls) for industrial action to which this notice relates and will give no support to unofficial industrial action taken in response to it (or them). If you are dismissed while taking unofficial industrial action, you will have no right to complain of unfair dismissal.

- Employers of those to whom the above notice is required to be given must also be given written notice of the fact and the date of the repudiation.
- An act is not, however, to be treated as having been repudiated if, at any time after the purported repudiation the president, general secretary or executive committee do anything inconsistent with that repudiation. A person who has a commercial contract (including a contract of employment) which was, or was liable to be, interfered with by the repudiated act is given certain rights. Such a person, if he has not already had notice that the act in question has been repudiated can, within

three months of the date of the repudiation, ask the union to confirm the repudiation in writing. If the union fails to provide written confirmation of the repudiation 'forthwith', this is to be treated as doing something inconsistent with the repudiation and thus will undermine the effect of the repudiation.

(iii)   Limit of trade union liability in tort
- Other than in relation to claims for:
  - personal injury arising out of negligence, nuisance or breach of duty
  - breach of duty in connection with the ownership, occupation, possession, control or use of property; and
  - product liability claims

the amount of damages awarded against a trade union in any action is limited by the size of the membership of the union.
- The limits are:

Number of members in union	Maximum damages
Fewer than 5,000	£10,000
5,000–25,000	£50,000
25,000–100,000	£125,000
100,000 or more	£250,000

- Amounts awarded by way of damages cost and expenses against
  - a trade union; or
  - trustees of union property, all the members of a trade union or the officials of a trade union when acting as such

cannot be recovered from 'protected property'.
- Protected property is:
  - property belonging to the trustees other than in their capacity as such
  - property belonging to any member of the union otherwise than jointly or in common with the other members
  - property belonging to an official of the union who is neither a member nor a trustee
  - property comprised in the union's political fund provided that, at the time of the action complained of, the fund was not allowed to be used for financing strikes or other industrial action
  - property comprised in a separate provident fund, including funds to provide benefits:
    - to members during sickness, incapacity from personal injury or accident
    - to members while out of work
    - by way of superannuation to aged members
    - to members who have lost their tools by fire or theft
    - for help with funeral expenses on the death of a member or the wife of a member
    - for making provision for the children of a deceased member.

(b) *Action taken in contemplation or furtherance of a trade dispute*
   (i)   Meaning of a trade dispute
- The definition of a 'trade dispute' for purposes of immunity from liability in tort in relation to industrial action is defined more strictly than it is defined in relation to the duties of ACAS (see 102.11(d) (i) above). In relation to industrial action and a union's immunity from action in tort, 'trade dispute' means a dispute between workers and their employer which relates wholly or mainly to one or more of the items that can be the subject of collective bargaining between a union and an employer (see *Collective bargaining* – 102.11 (a) (i) above).
- A dispute between a Minister of the Crown and any workers is to be treated as a trade dispute if it relates to matters that:
  - have been referred for consideration by a joint body on which the Minister is represented, or
  - cannot be settled without him exercising a statutory power.
- A trade dispute can relate to matters occurring outside the United Kingdom, so long as the people taking action in the United Kingdom are likely to be affected by the outcome of the dispute in respect of one or more of the matters on which a union can collectively bargain with their employer.

   (ii) Protection of action taken in contemplation or furtherance of a trade dispute
- One of the most important provisions of the Act is that, subject to certain limits, it provides that an act done by a person in contemplation of a trade dispute is not actionable in tort only on the grounds that it:
  - induces another person to break his contract; or
  - induces another person to interfere with the performance of a contract; or
  - threatens to do either of the above.
- This provision is important because it allows for industrial action to be called by a union and taken by employees without exposing them to the possibility of being sued for the torts of inducement to breach of contract, or interference with the performance of a contract.
- An *ex parte* injunction/interdict ('*ex parte*' means that the person against whom the claim is brought is not present or represented at the hearing) must not generally be granted where a person has claimed or is likely to claim that the action that it is sought to restrain is being taken in contemplation or furtherance of a trade dispute. The only exception is where the judge is satisfied that all reasonable steps have been taken to try to ensure that the defendant has had an opportunity of being heard before the application is decided.
- Where a court is asked to grant an interlocutory injunction in a case where a person claims, or is likely to claim, that the action was being

LIVERPOOL JOHN MOORES UNIVERSITY
LEARNING SERVICES

taken in contemplation or furtherance of a trade dispute, then it must consider the likelihood of that claim succeeding at the full trial before granting an injunction to restrain picketing or inducement to breach or interference with a contract. This does not extend to Scotland.

(iii) Peaceful picketing
- It is lawful for a person in contemplation or furtherance of a trade dispute to attend:
  - at or near his own place of work
  - where a person works at more than one place or if picketing at his place of work is impracticable, then he can attend at any of his employer's premises from which he works or from which his work is administered
  - if a worker has been dismissed in connection with a trade dispute or if the termination of his employment gave rise to a trade dispute, then he can attend at his former place of work; or
  - if he is a trade union official, at or near the place of work of a member of the union whom:
    - he is accompanying; and
    - whom he represents
  - for the purpose of peacefully:
    - obtaining or communicating information, or
    - persuading any person to work or abstain from working.
- The ACAS Code of Practice on picketing suggests that there should be a maximum of six pickets outside any place of work – although this requirement is advisory only.
- If picketing goes beyond what is allowed then the immunity from tortious liability is lost and pickets (and if the action is official, the unions) can be sued.

(iv) Actions specifically excluded from protection
- Action to enforce trade union membership
  - Any action that is taken
    - to enforce a trade union membership requirement for any employees or for people used on contracts; or
    - because an employer has used non-union people
    cannot be protected even if taken in contemplation or furtherance of a trade dispute.
- Action taken because of dismissal for taking unofficial action
  - An action loses its immunity if it relates, in whole or in part, to people being dismissed for taking unofficial industrial action.
- Secondary action
  - Secondary action occurs where a person
    - induces another to break a contract of employment
    - interferes with the performance of a contract of employment
    - induces another to interfere with its performance

- threatens that a contract of employment under which he or another is employed will be broken or its performance be interfered with; or
- threatens that he will induce another to break a contract of employment or to interfere with its performance

  where the employer under the contract of employment is not party to the dispute. Where there are a number of employers in dispute with their workers, each dispute between an employer and his workers is treated as a separate dispute.
  - Where action is primary action in one dispute (ie where the action is taken by workers against their own employer) then it cannot be outlawed as unlawful secondary action in relation to another dispute.
  - Secondary action (other than that which occurs in the course of lawful picketing) is not immune from action in tort.
- Action to impose union recognition
  - Action is not immune from suit in tort if it:
    - is taken to make those supplying goods or services use only union labour
    - is taken to try to stop someone obtaining a contract for goods or services because they use or will use non-union labour
    - interferes with the supply or goods or services and is taken by employees not employed by the supplier who believe that the supplier does not or might not recognise a union or consult or negotiate with a union.

(v) No order to compel work

It should be noted that even if unlawful action is taken by an employee no order for specific performance or injunction can be made by any court which would compel a person to work or to go anywhere to do work.

(c) *Ballot requirements before industrial action*

These provisions were extended considerably and amended by TURERA.

(i) General
- A trade union is not protected against liability for tort in relation to any industrial action unless that action has the support of a ballot; and
- a trade union is not protected in relation to any particular employer, in respect of industrial action, unless all proper notices and sample voting papers have been given to that employer.
- In the case of a workplace ballot, however, the action will be protected for that workplace if it has the support of a ballot and the proper notices and sample voting papers have been given to that employer which are valid for employees who work in the place of work in which the ballot is held.
- For an act to have the support of a ballot, all the requirements for a valid ballot and proper scrutiny of the ballot must be complied with.

(ii) Scrutiny of the ballot

- A scrutineer must be appointed to oversee an industrial action ballot unless
  - there are 50 or fewer employees who are being balloted; or
  - there are separate workplace ballots, the average number voting in each workplace ballot is 50 or fewer.
- In all other cases the trade union must:
  - appoint a scrutineer who is competent and of a type or from a list approved by the Secretary of State and who the union has no reason to believe will be biased
  - ensure that the scrutineer carries out his duties in relation to the ballot fully and that he is not subjected to any interference from any official, employee or member of the union in carrying out those functions
  - comply with all reasonable requests made by the scrutineer in carrying out his functions
  - where, within six months of the ballot a person who was entitled to vote in the ballot or an employer of any such person requests a copy of the scrutineer's report, provide one as soon as is practicable. (The union can make a reasonable charge for this.)
- The scrutineer's terms of appointment must require him:
  - to take such steps as appear to him to be appropriate for the purpose of enabling him to make a scrutineer's report to the union; and
  - to make the report as soon as is reasonably practicable after the date of the ballot and, in any event, within four weeks of the ballot.
- The scrutineer must make a report to the union, following the ballot, which states:
  - that there are no grounds for believing that there has been any breach of statute in relation to the ballot
  - that the arrangements for producing, storing and handling the voting papers used in the ballot, and the arrangements for the counting of the votes, were sufficiently secure to minimise any risk of unfairness or malpractice; and
  - that he has been able to carry out his functions without any interference from the union or any of its members, officials or employees.
  If he is not satisfied as to any of the above, then the report must say with what he is dissatisfied.
(iii) Notice of ballot
  - The union must ensure that the employers of those entitled to vote in the ballot receive:
    - not later than the seventh day before a voting paper is sent to anyone entitled to vote in the ballot (ie the 'opening day of the ballot'), a notice:
      - stating that the union intends to hold the ballot
      - stating the opening day of the ballot; and

- describing (so the employer can readily identify them) the employees whom the union reasonably believes will be entitled to vote in the ballot.
- not later than the third day before the 'opening day of the ballot' a sample voting paper which must be:
  - a sample of the form of voting paper that is to be sent to the employees who are entitled to vote in the ballot, or
  - where different employees are to be given different voting papers, a sample of each.

(iv) Entitlement to vote in ballot
  - Entitlement to vote in the ballot must be given to all the union's members whom the union believes will be induced to take part or continue to take part in the industrial action in question, and no one else.
  - The above requirement is to be taken not to have been satisfied if a person who was a union member at the date of the ballot and who was not given a vote is called upon to take industrial action.
  - Where members of a union have different places of work then separate workplace ballots must normally be held to ballot the members of the union working in each separate place of work, but
    - separate workplace ballots are not used where those who are given the right to vote in the ballot have some factor in common with other union members who are given the right to vote (though the factor they have in common need not be the same factor in each case – so, for example, all the staff employees or blue-collar employees over a number of sites could be balloted together).
      - The factor referred to above must be one that relates to the terms and conditions of those members' employment; or to the occupational description applicable to those members in their employment.
      - The factor must not be one that other employees who are not given a right to vote also have; or which individuals employed by that employer have in common because of their place of work.
  - Where a trade union has overseas members then it can decide whether or not to ballot them. Where it does, the scrutiny requirements and many of the other ballot requirements do not apply.

(v) The ballot
  - Voting must be by the voter marking a voting paper.
  - Each voting paper must:
    - state the name of the independent scrutineer where one is required
    - specify:
      - the date by which; and
      - the address to which the voting paper is to be returned
    - specify who is authorised to call upon members to take the industrial action if the vote is in favour of industrial action

- be marked with a unique number which is part of a consecutive series of numbers used for the ballot
- contain at least one of the following:
  - a question which requires the voter, by answering 'Yes' or 'No', to say whether he is prepared to take part or in a strike
  - a question which requires the voter, by answering 'Yes' or 'No', to say whether he is prepared to take part or in industrial action short of a strike
- contain the following statement (without qualification or comment):

  If you take part in a strike or other industrial action, you may be in breach of your contract of employment.

- Each person entitled to vote must
  - have a voting paper sent to him at his home or other mailing address
  - be given an opportunity to vote by post
  - be allowed to vote without interference from the union or any of its members, officials or employees; and
  - so far as is practicable be able to vote without incurring any cost to himself.
- A ballot must be conducted so that
  - so far as is practicable the voter can vote in secret; and
  - the votes in the ballot are fairly and accurately counted.
- As soon as is reasonably practicable, the union must ensure that those who were entitled to vote and their employers are informed of the numbers of:
  - votes cast
  - individuals answering 'Yes' to the question or to each question
  - individuals answering 'No' to the question or to each question
  - spoiled voting papers.
(vi) Calling industrial action
- For industrial action to have the support of a ballot:
  - it must be called by the person specified on the voting paper as having authority to call it
  - there must not have been any call to take the action before the date of the ballot; and
  - the industrial action must take place within four weeks beginning with the date of the ballot. Where a court prohibits or suspends the taking of industrial action for any time then the union can apply to the court to extend the period so it has a full, unconstrained, four weeks in which to take industrial action.
- For industrial action to be protected, the union must also ensure that the employer of anyone who will be called upon to take industrial action receives a notice of the action. This notice must not be given

before the results of the ballot have been sent to voting members, and must be received by the employer in question at least seven days before the industrial action referred to in the notice begins.

- The notice must:
  - identify the employees who are going to be called to take industrial action
  - state whether the action is intended to be continuous or discontinuous (ie whether once it starts it will take place on all the employees' working days or not) and
  - if continuous, state the intended date when any employees will start to take part
  - if discontinuous, state the dates when any employees will partake in the action
  - state that the notice is given for purposes of s 234A TULRA.

(d) *Action by an individual where goods or services are disrupted*

This provision was a major amendment to the law brought into effect by TURERA

The right

- Where, because of unlawful industrial action, whether actual or threatened, the supply of goods or services to an individual will or could be delayed or prevented, or the individual would not be able to get the same standard of goods or services, that individual may apply to a court. This applies whether or not the individual has a right to be supplied with those goods or services. Unlawful industrial action for these purposes is action which is actionable in tort by one or more persons, or which would entitle an individual trade union member to take action against the trade union in question (see *Rights of trade union members against the union* – 102.8 above). Where a court finds an action well founded it can grant an injunction/interdict to restrain further action being taken.

(e) *Dismissal of an employee while taking part in industrial action*

These provisions have been amended slightly by TURERA.

(i) Dismissal of those taking part in unofficial industrial action

- An employee has no right to claim unfair dismissal if at the time of dismissal he was taking part in unofficial industrial action.
- By an amendment brought in by TURERA this exclusion does not apply if the reason, or primary reason, for dismissal or for selection for redundancy was:
  - to do with maternity
  - to do with being a health and safety representative or safety committee member or taking action in a health and safety case; or
  - to do with being an employee representative.
- A strike will *not* be unofficial for these purposes if:
  - the person concerned is a trade union member and the action has been endorsed by his union

- the person concerned is not a trade union member, but some of the people taking action are trade union members and the action has been endorsed by their union; or
- none of the people taking part in the strike are trade union members.
- Note that for these purposes:
  - if an employee is a member of a trade union that is not connected to his employment this is to be disregarded; conversely if he was a member of a union when the action began, but thereafter ceased to be one, then he is deemed to have continued to be a union member
  - where an employee is dismissed with notice, the date of dismissal is the date when notice of dismissal is given
  - where the union repudiates any industrial action, that repudiation does not take effect to make the strike unofficial until the end of the next working day after the repudiation.

(ii)   Dismissal of those taking part in official industrial action
- An employment tribunal cannot determine the fairness or unfairness of an employee's dismissal if, at the date of dismissal:
  - the employer was conducting or instituting a lock-out; or
  - the complainant was taking part in strike or other industrial action
  unless one or more of the employees who were also involved in the industrial action or strike or were directly interested in the dispute giving rise to the lock-out ('relevant employees'):
  - have not been dismissed; or
  - have been offered re-engagement within three months of their dismissal, when the complainant has not.
- By an amendment brought in by TURERA this restriction does not apply if the reason, or primary reason for dismissal or for selection for redundancy was:
  - to do with maternity
  - to do with being a health and safety representative or safety committee member or taking action in a health and safety case; or
  - to do with being an employee representative.
- A complaint under this heading must be brought within six months from the date of the complainant's dismissal or, if that is not reasonably practicable, within such further time as is reasonably practicable.
- Where the complaint is of discriminatory re-engagement then the principal reason for dismissal for purposes of the ERA unfair dismissal/unfair selection for redundancy provisions and for purposes of dismissal/ selection for redundancy for trade union reasons under TULRA is the reason for which the complainant was not offered re-engagement.

(f) *Criminal charges arising out of industrial action*
  (i)   Breach of contract involving injury to persons or property
  - A person commits a criminal offence, punishable by a fine, if he

wilfully breaches his employment contract knowing or believing that the probable result of doing so (whether alone or with others) will be:
- to endanger life
- to cause serious bodily injury; or
- to expose real or personal property to destruction or serious injury.

(ii)   Intimidation or annoyance by violence or otherwise
- A person (the intimidator) commits a criminal offence, punishable by a fine, if to make another do or abstain from doing something which that person is legally entitled to choose to do or not to do (as he wishes), the intimidator
  - uses violence to, or intimidates, that person or his wife or children, or injures his property
  - persistently follows that person about from place to place
  - hides any tools, clothes or other property owned or used by that person, or deprives him of or hinders him in the use thereof
  - watches or besets the house or other place where that person resides, works, carries on business or happens to be, or the approach to any such house or place; or
  - follows that person with two or more persons in a disorderly manner in or through any street or road.

(iii)   Restrictions on the offence of conspiracy
In England and Wales
- Where an act that amounts to a criminal conspiracy which:
  - is done in contemplation or furtherance of a trade dispute; and
  - is a summary offence, not punishable with imprisonment

then it is not to be treated as a criminal conspiracy for purposes of prosecuting it as such.

In Scotland
- An agreement or combination by two or more persons to do, or procure to be done, an act in contemplation or furtherance of a trade dispute is not indictable as a conspiracy if that act committed by one person would not be punishable by imprisonment
- Where a person is found guilty of an offence which is punishable only on summary conviction, the maximum sentence is to be no more than three months or the statutory maximum that would apply if the offence had been committed by one person.

103   Trade Union and Labour Relations Acts 1974 and 1976

Originally the parts of these Acts relating to individual rights were repealed and consolidated into the Employment Protection (Consolidation) Act 1978. The Acts were further amended by the Employment Acts 1980 and 1982 with regard to collective matters (which were their only remaining sphere of operation). These provisions, as amended were consolidated into the TULRA.

104   Trade Union Reform and Employment Rights Act 1993 (TURERA)

This Act amended the Employment Protection (Consolidation) Act 1978, Transfer of Undertakings (Protection of Employment) Regulations 1981, Employment Acts 1980, 1982 and 1989 and the Trade Union and Labour Relations (Consolidation) Act 1992. The amendments to the EPCA have now been consolidated into the Employment Tribunals Act 1996 and the Employment Rights Act 1996. The provisions of this Act are examined under the statutes into which they have been consolidated or which they amend.

Amended by Employment Rights (Disputes Resolutions) Act 1998.

105   Transfer of Undertakings (Protection of Employment) Regulations 1981

Amended by TURERA, Collective Redundancies and Transfer of Undertakings (Protection of Employment) (Amendment) Regulations SI 1995/2587 and Transfer of Undertakings (Protection of Employment) (Amendment) Regulations 1999.

The Regulations were originally restricted to dealing with cases where a business, or part of a business, that was in the nature of a commercial venture was transferred from one person to another. This restriction, limiting the application of the Regulations to cases where the undertaking transferred was in the nature of a commercial venture was removed by TURERA to bring the Regulations into line with the EC Directive which they were introduced to implement. This means that the transfer of any undertaking is now covered by the Regulations, provided only that the undertaking was situated in the United Kingdom before the transfer and that the subject matter of the transfer is an 'undertaking' within this wider definition. TURERA further widens the ambit of what can amount to an undertaking by providing that no property need be passed from the transferor to the transferee for there to be a transfer under the Regulations. This makes it clear that the Regulations can cover the contracting-out of services by both commercial and non-commercial bodies – including government departments and local authorities – as well as the types of transaction which might more traditionally be viewed as a transfer of an undertaking. The major provisions of these Regulations are as follows.

105.1   Before the transfer

(a) *Consultation*

Originally the Regulations required employers to consult only where they recognised independent trade unions. The Collective Redundancies and Transfer of Undertakings (Protection of Employment) (Amendment) Regulations SI 1995/2587 now require consultation whether or not an independent trade union is recognised. Consultation is required in respect of all those employees who will be affected by the transfer. NB 'Employees affected' by the transfer are any employees in either the transferor undertaking (ie the seller), or the transferee undertaking (ie the buyer), who will be affected by the transfer. This does not apply merely to employees who will actually be transferred with the business.

(b) *Representatives for consultation*

These provisions have been significantly changed by the Collective Redundancies and Transfer of Undertakings (Protection of Employment) (Amendment Regulations) 1999 (SI 1999 No. 1925).

- An employer must allow employee representatives:
  - access to the employees whom it is proposed to make redundant
  - accommodation and such other facilities as may be appropriate; and
  - time off for training, taking part in elections, receiving information regarding the transfer and consulting about it.

(c) *Information to be given to employee representatives*

- Long enough before the transfer for consultations to take place, the employer must inform the employee representatives of:
  - the fact of the transfer and the reasons for it
  - the legal, economic and social implications of the transfer for the affected employees
  - the measures that he envisages taking with regard to those employees in connection with the transfer; and
  - if he is the transferor, any measures the transferee envisages taking (a duty is placed on the transferee to provide the necessary information in this respect).
- Where an employer envisages that he will be taking measures in connection with the transfer he must consult with employee representatives about these. TURERA modified the consultation required about measures to be taken in connection with transfer, so that the employer must now seek in these consultations to obtain agreement to the measures to be taken.

(d) *Compensation for failure to consult*

- If an employer fails to consult or to ensure that employee representatives are properly elected, an award can be made against him by an employment tribunal. The amount of the award will depend on the seriousness of the employer's failure and is subject to a maximum of 13 weeks' pay for each employee in respect of whom consultation should have taken place and did not. (TURERA raised the original level of two weeks' to four weeks'; the Collective Redundancies and Transfer of Undertakings (Protection of Employment) (Amendment) Regulations 1999 (SI 1999 No. 1925) have raised it further.)
- The appropriate claimant where an employer has not fulfilled the consultation requirements depends on the employer's particular failure. These have been amended by the Collective Redundancies and Transfer of Undertakings (Protection of Employment) (Amendment) Regulations 1999 (SI 1999 No. 1925). Where an employer has failed, the claim is made:
  - in the case of any failure relating to election of employee representatives,

by any of the affected employees or by any of the employees who have been dismissed as redundant
- in the case of any other failure relating to employee representatives, by any of the employee representatives to whom the failure relates
- in the case of any failure to fulfil any requirement relating to a trade union representative, by the trade union
- in any other case, by an affected employee or one who has been or may be dismissed as redundant.
- A claim must be brought within three months of the completion of the transfer (or if that is not reasonably practicable within such further period as is reasonably practicable).
- The Collective Redundancies and Transfer of Undertakings (Protection of Employment) (Amendment) Regulations 1999 (SI 1999 No. 1925) changed the burden of proof in relation to two situations. In both, the burden is put on to the employer:
  - in relation to the question of whether or not the employee representative was 'appropriate' the employer must prove that the employee representative had authority to represent the affected employees; and
  - it is for the employer to prove that the requirements concerning the election of employee representatives have been complied with.
- If the transferor claims that he has failed to provide information about the measures the transferee intended to take after the transfer because the transferee failed to provide him with that information, then:
  - he must notify the transferee of this claim; and
  - the transferee will then automatically be joined to the proceedings.

105.2   On transfer

(a) *Transfer of contracts*

The transferred employees' contracts are transferred with them and take effect as if they had been entered into with the transferee employer from the outset. An employee cannot leave and claim constructive dismissal unless either:

(i)   the change of ownership is a significant, detrimental, change for that employee; or

(ii)   the employee's conditions of work are substantially changed to his detriment.

By a TURERA amendment, however, an employee can leave when the undertaking is transferred, simply because he objects to becoming an employee of the transferee's. But if he does this he will not be treated as having been dismissed by either the transferor or the transferee.

(b) *Occupational pension schemes*

Occupational pension schemes are expressly excluded from transfer under these provisions. TURERA has amended this provision to make it clear that this restriction is confined strictly to pensions *per se*. If there are benefits within the pension scheme that are not themselves to do with 'old age, invalidity or survivors', then they are not to be treated as part of the pension scheme and would need to be preserved by the transferee.

(c) *Transfer of liability*
- All the transferor's civil liability to, or in connection with, the transferred employees is also transferred to the transferee, except in a case where the employee elects, 'on a whim', not to be transferred to the transferee (see (a) above).
- Criminal liability is specifically excluded from being transferred, but this would not prevent the transferee from becoming criminally liable immediately after the transfer for any offences that are continuing – such as continuing breaches of health and safety requirements.

(d) *Trade unions and collective agreements*
- Where an independent trade union was recognised before the transfer, and the part of the business transferred maintains a separate identity, then union recognition is transferred for that part of the business.
- Any collective agreement pertaining to a transferred employee is also transferred.

105.3   Unfair dismissal and redundancy

(a) It is *prima facie* automatically unfair to dismiss an employee because of a transfer unless there are economic, technical or organisational reasons entailing a change in the workforce in either transferor or transferee workforce. If there is such a reason, and that reason entails a change in the workforce, then the employer is treated as having a substantial reason for dismissal. The tribunal is then required, in terms of s 98(4) Employment Rights Act 1996, to decide whether or not the dismissal was fair. If the dismissal was fair then the employee will usually be entitled to a redundancy payment.

(b) If the employee leaves voluntarily upon transfer then, unless he can show that there has been a substantial change in his terms and conditions of employment which is to his detriment, he will not be entitled to a redundancy payment because he will not have been dismissed.

106   Truck Acts 1831–1940

Repealed by Wages Act 1986, which has itself been repealed and consolidated into the ERA.

Provided that all persons in manual employment (except domestic employees) be paid in 'coin of the realm'. This restriction was lifted by the Wages Act 1986. The Truck Acts also contained restrictions on deductions that might be made from the wages of such employees. These restrictions were amended and extended to all employees by the Wages Act 1986 and are now incorporated into the ERA.

107 Unfair Contract Terms Act 1977

Has relevance for employers who want to limit their liability to employees. Section 2 of the Act states:

(a) a person cannot, by reference to any contract terms or to a notice given to persons generally or to particular persons, exclude or restrict his liability for death or personal injury resulting from negligence;

(b) in the case of other loss or damage a person cannot so exclude or restrict his liability for negligence except in so far as the term or notice satisfies the requirement of reasonableness;

(c) where a term of a contract or a notice purports to exclude or restrict liability for negligence, a person's awareness of the term or notice is not of itself to be taken as indicating his voluntary acceptance of any risk.

107A Unfair Dismissal and Statement of Reasons for Dismissal (Variation of Qualifying Period) Order 1999 (SI 1999 No. 1436)

Amends the Employment Rights Act 1996.

These Regulations reduce the qualifying period for claiming unfair dismissal and entitlement to written reasons for dismissal from two years to one year with effect from 1 June 1999.

108 Wages Act 1986

Repeals Truck Acts 1831–1940, Payment of Wages Act 1960 and Wages Council Act 1979.

Amends Employment Protection (Consolidation) Act 1978.

Amended by Social Security Act 1986, Redundancy Rebates rights repealed by Employment Act 1989. The parts relating to Wages Council were repealed by Trade Union Reform and Employment Rights Act 1993.

The provisions re deductions from wages and payments by employees to employers were repealed and consolidated into the Employment Rights Act 1996.

108.1 Payment in 'coin of the realm'

The Wages Act 1986 repeals the Truck Acts' provisions insofar as they required that manual employees were paid in coin of the realm. Where employees have a contractual right to be paid in cash, the Payment of Wages Act 1960 (also repealed by the Wages Act 1986) allowed for employees to opt for payment otherwise than in cash. However, any such agreement could be revoked by the employee on giving four weeks' notice. The effect of the repeals brought about by the Wages Act 1986 is that an agreement for non-cash payment is now irrevocable.

108.2 Deductions from wages/payments to employees

These provisions have been consolidated into the Employment Rights Act 1996.

108.3   Wages Councils

The Wages Act 1986 repeals the Wages Councils Act 1979 and significantly reduced the functions and powers of the Wages Councils. Wages Councils were finally abolished by TURERA with effect from 30 August 1993.

108.4   Redundancy rebates

The Wages Act 1986 reduced the availability of redundancy rebates so that only small employers could still claim them. The Employment Act 1989 removed the last vestiges of the right to claim redundancy rebates.

109   Wages Councils Act 1979

Re-enacted the Wages Council Act 1959 as amended. This Act was repealed by the Wages Act 1986.

109A   The Working Time Regulations 1998 SI 1998 No 1833

Amend the Employment Rights Act 1996. These Regulations implement the Working Time Directive 93/104/EC and provisions concerning working time in the Protection of Young People at Work Directive 94/33/EC. The provisions of this Protection of Young People at Work Directive covered by the Regulations relate only to young people (ie those who are over compulsory school age and under 18). The provisions dealing with children's working hours are contained in the Children (Protection at Work) Regulations 1998 (SI 1998 No. 276) (see 9A above).

(a) *Who is covered*
  i)   The Regulations cover 'workers', who include:
   - all employees
   - all those who are under a contract to provide services personally other than in a case where the relationship is such that the 'employer' is the client or customer of the worker's business
   - 'agency workers'
   - non-employed trainees
   - the police and armed forces, but in relation to these sectors the Regulations are disapplied where the characteristics particular to these services inevitably conflict with these Regulations
  ii) Excluded sectors
   - The Regulations do not apply to adult workers in:
     - air, rail, road, sea, inland waterway and lake transport
     - sea fishing
     - any other work at sea
     - the activities of doctors in training; or
     - where the characteristics particular to certain specific activities of the civil protection services inevitably conflict with these Regulations

iii) Only the Regulations concerning rest breaks and annual leave apply to adults in domestic service

iv) Unmeasured working time
- Only the Regulations concerning health assessments for night workers, allowing breaks where the work is monotonous or runs at a pre-determined speed and paid annual leave apply to adults in the following categories:
  - managing executives and others with autonomous decision-taking powers
  - family workers
  - workers officiating at religious ceremonies in churches and religious communities
- Draft Regulations will provide that:
  - where part of an adult worker's working time is pre-determined or measured,
  - but the characteristics of the activity are such that, without being told by the employer to do so, he may also do work
    - of undetermined duration; or
    - which is determined by the worker himself

  then the Regulations concerning maximum working time, night work and health assessments in relation to night work apply only to that part of the worker's working time that is pre-determined or measured.

v) Other special cases

Subject to the requirement to provide compensatory rest (see (vii) below) the following requirements do not apply in relation to the categories of work and worker set out below.
- The excluded requirements are
  - average length of night work
  - the set length of night work where the work involves special hazards of heavy physical or mental strain
  - provisions for breaks during the day, daily rest period and weekly rest periods
- The categories of worker are adults:
  - whose place of work and residence, or different places of work, are distant from one another
  - engaged in security or surveillance where a permanent presence is required to protect property or persons – such as security guards or caretakers
  - in relation to whom there is a need for continuity of service or production, as may be the case in:
    - reception, treatment or care provided by hospitals or similar establishments, residential institutions and prisons
    - work at docks or airports

- press, radio, television, cinema production, postal and telecommunications services, civil protection services
- gas, water and electricity production and distribution; household refuse collection and incineration
- industries in which work cannot be interrupted on technical grounds
- research and development activities
- agriculture
- for whom there is a foreseeable surge of activity, as may be the case in relation to:
  - agriculture
  - tourism; and
  - postal services
- whose activities are affected by:
  - an occurrence due to unusual and unforeseeable circumstances, beyond the employer's control
  - exceptional events, the consequence of which could not have been avoided despite the exercise of all due care by the employer; or
  - an accident or the imminent risk of an accident

The Regulations are excluded in only two cases, in relation to young workers:

- those whose employment is covered by the Merchant Shipping Act 1995 are covered by different Regulations
- the requirements for rest breaks during the day and daily rest breaks do not apply where:
  - the employer requires a young worker to undertake work for which no adult is available
  - the work is occasioned by:
    - an occurrence due to unusual and unforeseeable circumstances, beyond the employer's control; or
    - exceptional events, the consequence of which could not have been avoided despite the employer exercising all due care
  - the work is of a temporary nature; and
  - the work must be performed immediately

  In any such case the employer must allow the young worker an equivalent period of compensatory rest within the following three weeks.

vi) Shift workers
- subject to the requirement to provide compensatory rest (see (vii) below)
  - the requirement for a daily break and for a weekly break do not apply where the worker cannot take a break of the requisite length because of a change of shift
  - the requirement for a daily break and for a weekly break do not apply to workers on 'split shifts' – whose work is split up over the day – as might be the case with cleaners or restaurant staff.

vii) Compensatory rest

   In certain cases (set out in the text) where the Regulations are disapplied, a worker who is not provided with the breaks he would otherwise be entitled to should, wherever possible, be given an equivalent period of compensatory rest. If it is not possible to give compensatory rest for objective reasons, the employer must afford the worker such protection as may be appropriate to safeguard the worker's health and safety.

(b) *Workforce agreements and collective agreements*

The concept of a 'workforce agreement' is one that is created by these Regulations.

- A workforce agreement must:
  - be in writing
  - last for a specified period not exceeding five years
  - apply:
    - to all the members of the workforce who do not have terms and conditions agreed under collective agreements; or
    - to all the members of the workforce of a particular group who do not have terms and conditions agreed under collective agreements
  - be signed by:
  - the duly elected representatives of the workforce or of the group; or
  - if the employer has not more than 20 workers by the majority of workers instead
  - be given by the employer to all the workers who are to be covered by it before the commencement date together with any guidance which they may need to understand it.
- There are certain rules set down concerning the election of representatives for the workforce:
  - the employer must decide on the number of representatives to be elected
  - the candidates for election must be relevant members of the workforce or relevant members of the group in respect of whom they seek election
  - no relevant member of the workforce or group may unreasonably be excluded from standing for election
  - all relevant members of the workforce or group must be entitled to vote
  - all relevant members must be given the right to vote for as many candidates as there are representatives to be elected
  - the election must be by secret ballot; and
  - the votes must be accurately counted.
- There is no specific remedy set down by the Regulations for any failure in the election of representatives of the workforce. But if there is a failure in the election process, the representatives would not be properly elected and the workforce agreement would therefore be void, leaving workers to claim rights under the Regulations as if the workforce agreement was not in place.

- A collective or workforce agreement can
  - modify or exclude any of the following requirements:
    - average length of night work
    - the set length of night work where the work involves special hazards of heavy physical or mental strain
    - the reference period for night workers
  - modify or exclude the right to breaks during the day, daily breaks and weekly breaks, but where the worker is required to work at a time that would otherwise be a rest break then he should, wherever possible, be given an equivalent period of compensatory rest (see (vii) above)

(c) *Maximum weekly working time*
  - i) General
    - Unless a worker has agreed in writing not to be subject to the maximum working time requirements, the worker must not work more than an average of 48 hours (inclusive of overtime) in each seven days of any reference period.
    - Subject to any different provisions in workforce or collective agreement, the reference period is either
      - each consecutive 17-week period; or
      - any period of 17 weeks in the course of the employee's employment.
    - Until a worker has been employed for 17 weeks the reference period is the amount of time for which he has been employed.
    - In the case of workers in 'Other Special cases' – (see (a) (v) above) – the reference period is 26 weeks.
    - Where there is a collective agreement or workforce agreement in place then the reference period agreed can be from 17 weeks to a maximum of 52 weeks.
  - ii) Average working time during each seven days of the reference period is calculated by using the following formula:

$$\frac{A + B}{C}$$

    - A is the worker's total working time during the reference period referable to that reference period
    - B is the number of days worked in the following reference period to make up for any 'excluded days' (see iii below) in the current reference period; and
    - C is the number of weeks in the reference period.
  - iii) 'Excluded days' are:
    - days off taken by the worker due to:
      - annual leave entitlement under the Regulations
      - sick leave
      - maternity leave; or

- any days during the reference period when the worker had agreed not to be subject to the maximum working time requirements.

   iv)   Agreement to exclude maximum
- At the time of writing, this requirement is in the process of being simplified so that the employer need only obtain the worker's agreement in writing; and
- keep up-to-date records of those who have agreed to exclude the maximum working time.

(d) *Night work*

   i)   Meaning of 'night time' and 'night worker'
- 'night time' is:
  - a period of at least seven hours which includes the period between midnight and 5.00 am
- the actual duration can be agreed by a contract of employment, workforce agreement or collective agreement
  - in the absence of an agreement, 'night time' is taken to be 11 pm to 6 am.
- A 'night worker':
  - normally works at least three hours at night during at least half his working days; or
  - is likely to work such a proportion of his time at night as may be specified by a workforce or collective agreement.

   ii)   Length of night work
- A night worker's normal hours of work in any reference period must not exceed an average of eight hours in each 24 hours and the employer must take all reasonable steps to ensure that this requirement is complied with.
- If the night worker's work involves special hazards or heavy physical or mental strain then his hours of work, when on night work, must not exceed eight in any 24-hour period. The worker's work involves special hazards or heavy physical or mental strain if:
  - it is identified as such in a workforce or collective agreement; or
  - it is recognised in a risk assessment under the Management of Health and Safety at Work Regulations 1992 as involving a significant risk to workers.
- The reference period for a night worker is either
  - each consecutive 17-week period; or
  - any period of 17 weeks in the course of the employee's employment.

Until a worker has been employed for 17 weeks, the reference period is the amount of time for which he has been employed.

Average normal working hours during each 24 hours in the reference period are calculated by using the following formula:

$$\frac{A}{B-C}$$

where
- **A** is the worker's total normal working hours during the reference period
- **B** is the number of days in the reference period; and
- **C** is the total number of hours during the reference period spent on weekly breaks (see below) by the worker, divided by 24.

iii) Health assessment of night workers
- General
  - Before assigning a worker to become a night worker the employer must ensure that the worker has the opportunity of a free health assessment unless the worker has had one previously and the employer has no reason to believe that it is no longer valid.
  - Night workers must be given the opportunity of regular free health assessments.
- Young workers
  - In the case of a young worker, the free assessments that are offered must include an assessment of the employee's capabilities; and
  - the requirement for health checks applies to a young worker in respect of work during the period from 10 pm to 6 am (known as the 'restricted period'):
    - ie it is not restricted to cases where the employee will become a night worker
    - but the provision does not apply if the work to which the young person is assigned is of an exceptional nature.
- A health assessment cannot be disclosed to the employer unless
  - the worker gives written consent to it being disclosed; or
  - the disclosure is restricted to a statement that the worker is fit to take up, or continue, night work.
- If a doctor advises an employer that a night worker is suffering from health problems associated with night work then the employer is obliged to transfer the worker to suitable work that is not 'night work', if it is available.

(e) *Records*
i) The employer must keep records that are adequate to show:
- compliance with the working time limits in relation to
  - the normal maximum average working week
  - the maximum average nightly hours of night workers
- which workers have opted out of the normal maximum average working week
- that the requirements for both initial and regular health assessments have been met in relation to night workers and young people working during the restricted period.

    ii)   These records must be kept for two years.

(f) *Rest breaks*

    i)   Rest breaks

- Where an adult worker's daily working time is more than six hours he is entitled to a rest break of not less than 20 minutes. A different length of break can be agreed in a workforce or collective agreement.
- Where a young person's daily working time is more than four and a half hours he is entitled to a rest break of not less than 30 minutes. (If a young person is employed by more than one employer on any day his working time over the whole day must be added together for purposes of ascertaining whether or not he is entitled to a break.)

    ii)   Patterns of work

- Where the work that is being done by the worker is monotonous or the work rate is pre-determined, the worker must be given adequate breaks to ensure his health and safety.

    iii)   Daily rest

- An adult is entitled to at least 11 consecutive hours' rest in each 24.
- A young worker is entitled to at least 12 consecutive hours' rest in each 24; however, this period may be interrupted if the work being done is split up over the day or is of short duration.

    iv)   Weekly rest period

- An adult worker is entitled to an uninterrupted rest period of:
  - 24 hours in each seven-day period
  - two periods of 24 hours in each 14-day period; or
  - 48 hours in each 14-day period.
- This period is not to include the 11 hours daily rest break that an adult is entitled to each day unless this is justified by
  - objective reasons
  - technical reasons; or
  - reasons concerning the organisation of work.
- A young worker is entitled to an uninterrupted rest period of not less than 48 hours in every seven-day period but:
  - this may be interrupted where the work involves periods of work which are:
    - split up over the day; or
    - are of short duration
  - this may be reduced to no fewer than 36 consecutive hours where this is justified by organisational or technical reasons.

(g) *Entitlement to annual leave*

    i)   General

- An employee who has been continuously employed for at least 13 weeks is entitled to four weeks' paid leave in each leave year beginning on or after 23 November 1999.

- If no leave year is agreed either in the worker's contract of employment or in a workforce or collective agreement, then the leave year starts on
  - 1 October if the employee was employed on or before on 1 October 1998; or
  - the date when the employee started in employment, if later.
- If the employee is employed for only part of any leave year, then the entitlement is *pro rata* with any part days' entitlement being rounded up to full days' leave.

ii) Dates on which leave is taken
- Leave may be taken in instalments, but it can be taken only in the leave year in respect of which it is due.
- Where the worker wants to take any period of leave he must give the employer notice of at least twice the length of the period of leave that he wishes to take.
- If the employer wants to
  - prevent the worker from taking leave at any particular time; or
  - make the worker take leave at a particular time
  then this can be done by the employer giving notice of the same length as the amount of leave in question.
- The notice, in either case:
  - may relate to all or only some of the worker's annual leave entitlement
  - must specify the days on which leave is or is not to be taken; and
  - if the leave is for only part of the day – it must give the duration of that leave.
- These notice provisions can be changed by the contract of employment, by specific agreement with an employee or by a workforce or collective agreement.

iii) Payment in respect of periods of leave
- Where the worker is entitled to leave under these provisions then payment for the leave is calculated on the basis of the statutory 'week's pay'; the calculation date being the first day of the worker's leave.
- Any contractual remuneration is set off against any payment that would otherwise be due under the Regulations.
- Other than on termination of employment, no payment can be made in lieu of statutory annual leave entitlement.
- On termination of employment the worker is entitled to be paid *pro rata* for any leave not taken.
- Provision can be made in a contract of employment, by specific agreement with an employee, or by a workforce or collective agreement, to allow the employer to recoup payment or to have work done by the worker to compensate for any leave taken by the worker in excess of his entitlement, on termination.

(h) *Entitlement under Regulations and other provisions*
Workers who have rights to rest periods, rest breaks or annual leave under the provisions of the Regulations and under a separate provision, for example their contracts, cannot exercise both rights separately, but can 'pick and mix' the rights to obtain the best single composite rights.

(i) *Legal remedies to enforce the Regulations*
  i) Enforcement
  - Enforcement of the Regulations is by:
    - the Health and Safety Executive; or
    - the local authority which is responsible for enforcing health and safety matters in relation to certain premises under the Health and Safety (Enforcing Authority) Regulations 1998 (SI 1998 No. 494).
  - Failure to comply with any of the provisions of the Regulations is a criminal offence.
  ii) Claim to employment tribunal
  - An employee can complain to an employment tribunal where the employer has failed to
    - provide proper rest breaks or daily or weekly rest periods
    - provide annual leave entitlement; or
    - pay for annual leave entitlement.
  - A claim must be made within three months (or in the case of a complaint from members of the armed forces, within six months) of:
    - the day or the first day of
      - any rest period; or
      - period of annual leave; or
    - the day on which payment for any period of annual leave should have been made.

    There is the usual provision for extension of time if it is not reasonably practicable for the worker to present the claim within the normal period.
  iii) Right not to suffer detriment or to be unfairly dismissed
  - Workers are entitled not to be unfairly dismissed for asserting a statutory right in relation to the Regulations for:
    - having brought proceedings to enforce any right under the Regulations; or
    - having alleged that the employer has infringed any such right.
  - Provided the allegation is made in good faith it does not matter
    - whether the worker has the right alleged to have been infringed; or
    - whether it was infringed.
  - Workers are entitled not to suffer a detriment or to be unfairly dismissed because the worker:
    - refused, or proposed to refuse:
      - to comply with any request that the employer wanted to impose in contravention of the Regulations
      - to forgo any right given to him under the Regulations

- failed to sign a workforce agreement or to enter into any other agreement allowed for by the Regulations
- performed or proposed to perform any functions or activities as:
  - a representative of the workforce for purposes of a workforce agreement; or
  - a candidate for election as a workforce representative.

iv) Restrictions on contracting out
- The Regulations can be contracted out of only to the extent allowed for by the Regulations themselves.
- The normal provisions apply allowing for compromise agreements and settlement via ACAS of any claims.

110 Workplace Health, Safety and Welfare Regulations (SI 1992 No. 3004)

This is one of the 'Six-pack' Regulations introduced in 1992 arising from European health and safety directives. The Regulations amend the Offices, Shops and Railway Premises Act 1963 and the Factories Act 1961.

These Regulations are concerned with the premises provided for employees to work in and with the fixtures, fittings and services, such as heating, ventilation, sanitary facilities, etc. that are part of those premises. The requirements under these regulations include:

(a) *Ventilation*
Adequate ventilation must be provided. Where adequate ventilation is maintained by a machine which, if it broke down, would create a health and safety risk, an audible or visible alarm must be fitted to the machine to signal any breakdown.

(b) *Temperature*
The temperature in a workplace must be reasonable during working hours and an adequate number of thermometers must be provided to enable people to know what the temperature in the workplace is.

(c) *Lighting*
The lighting in a workplace must be suitable and sufficient and, so far as is reasonably practicable, should be natural light. Where there would be special hazards in a workplace if the lighting were to fail then emergency lighting must be provided.

(d) *Cleanliness*
The furniture and fittings in a workplace must be kept clean and waste must not be allowed to accumulate in the workplace (other than in suitable receptacles).

(e) *Working space*
There should be approximately 11 cubic metres of room space per person, although this may need to be increased if furniture or other fittings take up a lot of space in the workplace.

(f) *Work station*
  (i)   Every workstation must be:
        - adequately protected from bad weather
        - designed to ensure that the employee/s can leave quickly, or be assisted away in the case of an emergency
        - designed to ensure that the person working there will not slip or fall.
  (ii) Where work can or must be done sitting down then a suitable seat, and where necessary a suitable footrest, should be provided.

(g) *Floors and traffic routes*
  (i)   Floors and traffic routes
        - must be suitably constructed for the purpose for which they are used
        - must not have holes in them or be slippery or uneven.
  (ii) The workplace must be organised so that pedestrians and vehicles can circulate in a safe manner.
  (iii) Escalators and moving walkways must:
        - function safely
        - be equipped with necessary safety devices
        - be fitted with an easily identifiable, easily accessible, emergency stop control.

(h) *Windows and doors*
  (i)   Windows and other translucent materials in walls and doors must be made of safety material to prevent breakage and should be marked to ensure that people realise that the material is there.
  (ii) Windows and skylights that can be opened must not be in a position such that opening them could give rise to a health and safety hazard.
  (iii) All windows and skylights must be designed or constructed so that they can be cleaned safely.
  (iv) Doors and gates must be suitably constructed and have any necessary safety devices, in particular:
        - sliding doors must have a device to prevent them coming off their tracks; and
        - upward opening doors must have a device to prevent them falling down.

(i) *Falling, and falling material*
There must be adequate protection against employees' falling or being struck by falling objects. Particular care must be taken to prevent employees from falling into or being struck by any dangerous substance (ie one that might burn or scald or which is poisonous, suffocating or corrosive, or which by its mere volume is likely to cause danger if it escapes). Adequate protection may include fencing or covering dangerous materials and making adequate safety provision where work is being carried out on ladders or scaffolds or where materials are stored high up. The protection envisaged by this Regulation is not the provision of personal protective equipment, training or information about the danger unless no other protection is possible.

(j) *Sanitary conveniences, washing facilities and changing facilities*
  (i) An adequate number of sanitary conveniences and washing facilities must be provided
    - where the number of employees is less than five, then only one WC and one washing facility need be provided
    - a second WC and washing facility is required when the number reaches 25; and
    - an extra WC and washing facility should be provided for each additional 25 employees thereafter.
  (ii) Showers may also be required by the nature of the work.
  (iii) Washing facilities must have hot and cold or warm water available.
  (iv) Where employees change into different clothes for work, adequate facilities must be made available:
    - to keep clothes secure
    - to separate work and personal clothes where this is necessary in health and safety terms; and
    - to allow clothes to be dried where possible.
  (v) Where employees need to change into different clothes for work, adequate changing facilities must be made available for them.
(k) *Facilities for rest, eating meals and drinking water*
  (i) Suitable and sufficient rest facilities must be provided:
    - where necessary for health and safety
    - in which to eat food if:
      - food would otherwise become contaminated when eaten at work; or
      - where food is regularly eaten at the workplace.
    - Rest areas must have suitable arrangements to protect non-smokers from tobacco smoke.
    - Suitable rest facilities must be provided for pregnant women and nursing mothers.
  (ii) There must be an adequate supply of drinking water, which is readily accessible to employees.

111 Young Persons (Employment) Acts 1938 and 1964

Repealed by the Employment Act 1990.

Index

LIVERPOOL JOHN MOORES UNIVERSITY
Aldham Roberts L.R.C.
TEL. 051 231 3701/3634